921
BU

Kilian, Pamela

Barbara Bush

$19.95

Barbara Bush

ALSO BY PAMELA KILIAN

What Was Watergate?

Pamela Kilian

Barbara Bush:
A
BIOGRAPHY

St. Martin's Press ■ New York

Grateful acknowledgment is made for permission to reprint from the following:

"Parenting's Best-Kept Secret: Reading to Your Children," by Barbara Bush, *Reader's Digest*, October 1990. Copyright © 1990 by The Reader's Digest Assn., Inc.

Recipes from "Barbara Bush Hosts a Tea Party," reprinted from *McCall's* magazine. Copyright © 1986 by the New York Times Company.

Design by Judith A. Stagnitto

Library of Congress Cataloging-in-Publication Data

Kilian, Pamela.
    Barbara Bush : a biography / Pamela Kilian.
      p.   cm.
    "A Thomas Dunne book".
    ISBN 0-312-07649-5
    1. Bush, Barbara, 1925–   .   2. Bush, George, 1924–   .
3. Presidents—United States—Wives—Biography. I. Title.
E883.B87K55   1992
973.928'092—dc20
[B]   92-3363
                                        CIP

First Edition: June 1992
10 9 8 7 6 5 4 3 2 1

Acknowledgments

Although I was not able to interview Barbara Bush for this book, her White House Press Office was of great help to me, especially Press Secretary Anna Perez.

Mrs. Bush's childhood companions—June Biedler, Rosanne Morgan Clarke, and Kate Siedle—provided much of the detail about her younger years, while Ashley Hall friends—Cordelia Stites, Shavaun Robinson Towers, Marjorie Macnutt Thurstone, Susan Estes Edgerly, Frances Baker Turnage, Mariam House, and Jane Thornhill—filled me in on her adolescence.

Special thanks to Otha Taylor for her story about traveling across country with Mrs. Bush during the era of segregation.

Three of Mrs. Bush's close friends—Mary Ann (Andy) Stewart, Shirley Pettis Roberson, and Betsy Heminway—were very helpful, as was Becky Beach, Mrs. Bush's traveling companion during the 1980 campaign.

Thanks also to Janet Steiger, Jessica Catto, Patsy Caulkins, Pete Teeley, Edward Derwinski, and W. Tapley Bennett.

And finally, thanks to my husband, Michael, for insights gleaned from covering Mrs. Bush over the years, for the *Chicago Tribune*.

Contents

Barbara Bush

Introduction

Barbara Bush was walking through an airport one day with two close friends when she was approached by a woman who gave her a big hug and a kiss.

"Who is that?" one of the women accompanying Barbara asked the other.

"Oh, just one of Bar's four thousand best friends," the second woman replied.

This story is told with amusement by Janet Steiger, one of the four thousand. Janet's friendship with Barbara Bush dates from the late 1960s, when both were active in a Republican congressional wives' club right after their husbands were elected to Congress for the first time.

But Barbara has friends from even earlier periods of her life—the long years she spent in Texas, her one year at Smith College, her finishing school in South Carolina, and her childhood in Rye, New York.

People who worked for her years ago—housekeepers, aides, nannies—still speak of her fondly, and most still get cards and pictures from her. She has had the same housekeeper for several decades.

The same personality traits—warmth, self-confidence, intelligence, and a natural outgoing style—that sustain Barbara

Bush's friendships have made her an enormously popular First Lady.

But she thinks the term "First Lady" is silly, and she doesn't like too much gushy praise. During her second year in the White House, a number of newspaper articles about her popularity came out. Finally Barbara refused to be interviewed by a reporter who wanted to do another one.

"Doesn't she like stories about her popularity?" the reporter asked.

"They make her want to throw up," Press Secretary Anna Perez replied.

Many of the stories portrayed her as a grandmotherly type, kind of warm and fuzzy and much like a next-door neighbor. Eventually she felt compelled to dispel the idea that she is "just folks."

"People write to me and say, 'I know I could talk to you.' And they could. And I could talk to them," she told the *Ladies Home Journal* in 1990. "But," she added pointedly, "I could also talk to the Queen of England. Or maybe I shouldn't use her as an example, but Margaret Thatcher, or Deng Xiaoping. Or Mrs. Sadat."

The point is well taken. Even if Barbara had not grown up in a monied community and gone to finishing school and a top women's college, she has gained experience and stature during a quarter century in public life. She has met almost all the world's leaders and their wives and has socialized with many of them, achieving an amicable relationship with such varying personalities as Raisa Gorbachev and Nancy Reagan. She is comfortable mugging for the camera with Denis Thatcher and telling funny stories about the eating habits of an African potentate.

Barbara has always been popular. When she was in elementary school, she had the nasty habit of arranging freeze-outs of girls in her circle, so that some unsuspecting soul would get on the school bus in the morning and find no one speaking to her. But this didn't lead to her expulsion from the group; the girls just wanted to stay on her good side.

(During her early years in Washington she regaled friends with imitations of pompous pols, but friends swear she was never vicious about it.)

In her teen years, she was pretty and vivacious and never lacked for male attention. But her storybook romance with George Bush pushed aside any interest she had in other boys.

Underneath her self-deprecating humor, Barbara Bush is a strong woman. She grew up in the shadow of a beautiful older sister who was favored by her somewhat distant mother, and the two women dominated her life until the day she married. From the posh suburbs of Rye she moved to the wilds of Texas with her young husband, thousands of miles from home and family. She thrived, and when his job took them to California and five moves in a single year, she didn't complain. She organized each home and raised the children while he traveled all week long.

Barbara was pregnant and in California when her mother died in a freak accident; she didn't go to the funeral, a decision she says she still regrets.

Her relationship with her good-humored father was much easier. He always took her side and she in turn adored him.

Since her marriage, Barbara became as close to George's family as to her own. In some cases, relations were even closer. She had an easier relationship with Mrs. Bush than with her own mother, and summer visits to Walker's Point in Kennebunkport were always a pleasure for her because the Bush family usually spent the season there.

During George Bush's early years in Washington, Barbara got little public attention, which was fine with her. But she had to face bigger and bigger crowds when he ran for president in the late 1970s and when he became Ronald Reagan's running mate in 1980.

In those days she had some rocky moments dealing with questions she didn't want to answer, and she got prickly when anyone criticized her husband. Sometimes her quick wit seemed offensive.

But Barbara always knew when she was making a bad

impression, and her skills at news conferences and on the campaign trail have increased over the years.

Now, as she says, she can talk easily to most any voter, to most any head of state, and to any audience in the world. She is as comfortable in the public eye as any elected politician— and more adept at making the most of her position than many of them.

This book is the story of how she got that way.

1

Wowing Wellesley

*B*arbara Bush dropped out of college in her sophomore year to marry the first man she had ever kissed. Now, forty-six years later, she was sitting in a huge white tent at Wellesley College's graduation ceremonies, ready to give a commencement address to a group of young women who had questioned her credentials.

She didn't apologize for her lack of formal education or express regret that she had no career. Instead, she stood up for the values that have shaped her life—loyal wife, loving mother, cheerful homemaker, and volunteer worker.

"For several years, you've had impressed upon you the importance to your career of dedication and hard work, and of course that's true," she told the 1990 graduating class. "But as important as your obligations as a doctor, a lawyer, a business leader will be, you are a human being first, and those human connections with spouses, with children, with friends are the most important investment you will ever make.

"At the end of your life, you will never regret not having passed one more test, winning one more verdict, or not closing one more deal. You will regret time not spent with a husband, a child, a friend, or a parent."

These sentiments were not the predominant ones at Wellesley in 1990, as Barbara was well aware. She noted that for more than fifty years it had been said the winner of the school's annual hoop race would be the first to get married; now it was said the winner would be first to head a major company.

"Both of those stereotypes show too little tolerance," Barbara said. "So I want to offer a new legend. The winner of the hoop race will be the first to realize her dream—not society's dreams—her own personal dream.

"Who knows?" she said. "Somewhere out in this audience may even be someone who will one day follow in my footsteps and preside over the White House as the president's spouse."

She paused.

"And I wish him well."

The six hundred Wellesley graduates and five thousand friends and relatives loved it. They laughed and clapped, giving Barbara a hearty ovation.

She had won them over with humor and honesty, a refusal to pretend to be something she wasn't, but also an acknowledgment that members of the Class of 1990 at Wellesley might make different choices from those of the Class of '47 at Smith College—which Mrs. Bush would have been part of if she hadn't quit school to marry George Bush.

The fact that she had dropped out and become famous because of her husband's accomplishments had bothered some of the Wellesley seniors.

At Wellesley, the commencement speaker is chosen by popular vote. Novelist Alice Walker had been first choice, but she refused. Barbara Bush was second choice; she accepted.

Two of the seniors, Susana Cardenas and Peggy Reid, were so unhappy with this outcome that they circulated a petition several months before graduation asking the Wellesley administration to reconsider the invitation.

"Wellesley teaches that we will be rewarded on the basis of

our own merit, not that of a spouse," the petition said. "To honor Barbara Bush as a commencement speaker is to honor a woman who has gained recognition through the achievements of her husband, which contradicts what we have been taught over the last four years at Wellesley."

About 150 women—25 percent of the senior class—signed the petition. When reporters arrived on campus to ask questions, Susana Cardenas told them that Barbara Bush was "the farthest she can be from the ideals of a progressive, feminist institution where you're taught to work hard to be recognized for your own contributions. If she hadn't been married to this guy who happens to be president, we never would have heard of her."

When word of the protest got around, it caused a national debate, with almost everyone lining up on Barbara's side.

The president was one of her stoutest defenders.

"I think that these young women can have a lot to learn from Barbara Bush and from her unselfishness and from her advocacy of literacy and of being a good mother and a lot of other things," he said when asked about the controversy.

Barbara herself understood the protesters' objections and accepted them for what they were. "I think George cared much more than I did," she said.

But she added, "I don't think they understand where I'm coming from, and that's all right. I chose to live the life I've lived and I think it's been a fabulously exciting, interesting, involved life. I hope some of them will choose the same exciting, interesting, fulfilling, involved life. In my day, they probably would have been considered different. In their day, I'm considered different. *Vive la différence.*"

Not everyone shared Barbara's charitable view. During her fifteen months as First Lady, she had grown increasingly popular, and many people considered the protest an insult.

"I'd like to spank some of those young women," said Carol Johnson Johns, a medical professor and one-time acting president of Wellesley. "I think they're missing the boat if they don't appreciate the satisfaction and fulfillment of a significant relationship with someone important to you and with your family, as well as the things you can contribute as a volunteer. . . . I think to put her down because she doesn't have a professional degree or a professional career is a miscarriage of value systems."[1]

Martha Church, a Wellesley alumna and president of Hood College, said the seniors appeared to be "seeing Barbara Bush in terms of the one issue that's most prominent on their minds—getting that first job that they've prepared for. I hear them, but I think they're ignoring another important side of themselves—their role as a volunteer, and her role as a volunteer. She's exemplary, in my view, of the qualities I hope will be instilled in our undergraduates—generousness of spirit."[2]

Some alumnae pointed out archly that the young protesters apparently had forgotten Wellesley's Latin motto: *"Non ministrari, sed ministrare,"* meaning "Not to be served, but to serve."

Barbara also drew a strong defense from editorial writers and newspaper columnists—even those who are frequently critical of George Bush.

"Those young women are probably right when they say that except for her marriage, the country would never have heard of Barbara Bush," the *New York Times* said in an editorial. "She'd be just one more of those millions of unsung Americans, female and male, who believe that raising decent children is the most important job. But these young women are wrong when they question Mrs. Bush's self-affirming qualities. She has said she's never regretted the choice she made at 19, and to contemplate the life she's made for herself and her family is to know she's telling the truth. By most people's lights Barbara Bush has been self-affirming all along."[3]

Syndicated columnist Ellen Goodman of the *Boston Globe* thought the young graduates were expressing anxiety about their own lives by objecting to Barbara Bush—and what she stood for—as a speaker.

"So in many ways, this may be a proper match for a commencement day," Goodman said. "In the audience, a class of women with diplomas as fresh as a new deck of cards. Each holding 52 options, wondering which ones to play, how many at once and whether it's easiest at solitaire. On the podium, a woman who took some of the cards that were dealt her and rearranged them into the best order. A woman who has played her hand with grace and character."[4]

Back at Wellesley, there were attempts to defuse the controversy. Nan Keohane, the school's president, said the protest was not unusual and had been blown out of proportion.

"Every year we have students who don't like the choice of speaker and every year somebody signs a petition," she said, adding that the flap over Mrs. Bush was "largely a generational thing."

Wellesley's class president, Julie Porter, came to the First Lady's defense. "I support Mrs. Bush coming here," she said. "She's a very interesting and successful lady who lived in a different time."

The two students who initiated the petition were overwhelmed by the response, which sometimes turned ugly. Susana Cardenas, who at first was the most outspoken against the Bush choice, received threatening telephone calls and letters telling her to go back to Peru, her native land.

The other main backer of the protest, Peggy Reid, expressed her outrage over the reaction in an article in the *New York Times*. Ms. Reid did what people under siege often do—she blamed the press for her troubles:

"All right, I've had enough," she said. "As a Wellesley college student and co-author of the petition that started this whole Barbara Bush mess, I'd like to set the record straight.

"Over the past month and a half, I have witnessed an outrageous perversion of what in reality is a very simple issue of discontent over Barbara Bush's speaking at this year's commencement exercises.

"The media have succeeded in creating a sensation by misrepresenting and misconstruing our original position. They have vastly misled the general public. Not once have we condemned the first lady for her role as a mother and a volunteer. We are not, as some would have you believe, 'careerists' who look down their noses at any woman who does not hold a paying job. . . .

"We do not advocate, as a commentator in the *Boston Globe* put it, 'a vision of feminism defined exclusively as success in the world of traditional masculine work.' Please don't be misled: Wellesley students did not miss the point in Feminism 101!

"So what was it we were protesting when we wrote a petition that called Barbara Bush an inappropriate commencement speaker? If we support motherhood and volunteer work, what is it that we have against Barbara Bush as a commencement speaker?

"The plain and simple fact is that Barbara Bush was not chosen as a speaker because of her commendable role as a mother; nor was she chosen for her admirable volunteer work. If such were the case, why were other equally dedicated mothers and community volunteers not chosen? The bottom line is that these women are not married to George Bush.

"Barbara Bush was selected because of her husband's accomplishments and notoriety, not those of her own. So it is not the validity of her choices in life that we are calling into question, but rather that fact that we are honoring not Barbara Bush, but Mrs. George Bush."[5]

Ms. Reid's article did nothing to quell the debate. Most people understood what the protest was about, and they rejected the arguments.

"Of those highbrow Wellesley seniors who object to Barbara Bush's forthcoming commencement appearance on the grounds she was invited because she is 'George's wife,' I wonder how many were able to afford four years of tuition, room and board at this costly, exclusive New England college only because they are 'daddy's daughter,' " a reader wrote to the *Los Angeles Times*.[6]

But Barbara continued to defend Wellesley against critics. "The poor girls, they're so bored with it now they could throw up," she said.

"I've gotten so many letters about Wellesley from people saying, 'I'm never going to give to Wellesley again.' I'd like to write a letter saying, 'Please give to Wellesley.' This is very normal. I understand it. It's no big deal. I mean, I'm very sorry that it all happened. Well, there are them who don't approve of me and them that do. But I'm just sorry for Wellesley."[7]

About two weeks before the commencement, the White House announced that Barbara Bush would be accompanied to Wellesley by Raisa Gorbachev, wife of the Soviet president, since the Gorbachevs would be in Washington that week for a summit meeting.

The news guaranteed that Wellesley's commencement would be in the national spotlight, and it put more pressure on Barbara. Raisa Gorbachev has an advanced college degree and has taught at the college level, a fact noted in a rather graceless way by one Wellesley senior.

"I'm really excited," senior Angie Hickman said of Mrs. Gorbachev's appearance. "She might have something more interesting to say."[8]

The day of the speech, June 1, was hot and sunny. On campus, the ill-will that preceded the event was muted, but it had not disappeared. About a third of the seniors wore purple armbands, which they explained—in letters left on all five thousand folding chairs—were to "celebrate all the unknown women who have dedicated their lives to the service of others."

The fuzzy symbolism of the armbands didn't detract from the festive atmosphere, though; it was the first time the wives of the presidents of the United States and the Soviet Union had shared a public podium, and the day had the exultant feel of history in the making. When Mrs. Bush and Mrs. Gorbachev arrived, accompanied by both Secret Service and KGB agents, the applause was thunderous.

Barbara spoke first. She started with acknowledgments and praise for Wellesley. Then she told a little story about the importance of tolerance, quoting from a speech given a year earlier at Smith College by the student body president.

The young woman had related a tale told by writer Robert Fulghum about a young pastor who thought up a game called "Giants, Wizards, and Dwarfs" for a group of children in his care.

"You have to decide now," the pastor instructed the children, "which you are—a giant, a wizard, or a dwarf?"

At that, a small girl tugging at his pants leg asked, "But where do the mermaids stand?" And the pastor tells her there are no mermaids. And she says, "Oh, yes there are. I am a mermaid."

"Now this little girl knew what she was, and she was not about to give up on either identity or the game," Barbara said. "She intended to take her place wherever mermaids fit into the scheme of things. Where do the mermaids stand—all of those who are different, those who do not fit the boxes and the pigeonholes? 'Answer that question,' wrote Fulghum, 'and you can build a school, a nation or a whole world.' "

Barbara continued: "As that very wise young woman said, 'Diversity, like anything worth having, requires effort.' Effort to learn about and respect difference, to be compassionate with one another, to cherish our own identity, and to accept unconditionally the same in others. You should all be very proud that this is the Wellesley spirit."

It was the most gracious of rebukes, an acknowledgment of the months of controversy, and a clear statement of how Barbara Bush felt about it.

She followed up immediately with a lighthearted remark that left everyone laughing happily.

"Now I know your first choice today was Alice Walker—guess how I know—known for *The Color Purple*. Instead you got me, known for the color of my hair!"

This brought wild applause, and Barbara turned to the heart of her message.

"As you set off from Wellesley, I hope many of you will consider making three very special choices. The first is to believe in something larger than yourself, to get involved in some of the big ideas of our time. I chose literacy because I honestly believed that if more people could read, write, and comprehend, we would be that much closer to solving so many of the problems that plague our nation and our society.

"And early on I made another choice, which I hope you will make as well. Whether you are talking about education, career, or service, you are talking about life and life really must have joy. It's supposed to be fun. One of the reasons I made the most important decision of my life, to marry George Bush, is because he made me laugh. It's true, sometimes we laugh through our tears, but that shared laughter has been one of our strongest bonds.

"Find the joy in life," she said, "because as Ferris Bueller said on his day off: 'Life moves pretty fast and if you don't stop and look around once in a while you are going to miss it.' "

This reference to one of the day's popular movies got huge applause. Barbara deadpanned, "I am not going to tell George you clapped more for Ferris than you clapped for George."

Turning serious again, she told the seniors her third choice in life had been to make her family and friends paramount, to cherish the human connections.

"Whatever the era, whatever the times, one thing will never change," she said. "Fathers and mothers, if you have children, they must come first. You must read to your children and you must hug your children and you must love your children. Your success as a family, our success as a society, depends not on what happens in the White House, but on what happens inside your house."

While stressing these traditional family values, Barbara also acknowledged the changes that have occurred in the four decades since she was a young college woman with a prediction that a woman would be president some day.

As laughter and applause filled the tent, she alluded to the weeks of tension that preceded the graduation.

"The controversy ends here, but our conversation is only beginning," she said, "and a worthwhile conversation it has been. So, as you leave Wellesley today, take with you deep thanks for the courtesy and the honor you have shared with Mrs. Gorbachev and with me."

Wellesley gave Barbara an enthusiastic standing ovation, then settled down to hear the Soviet First Lady speak.

Mrs. Gorbachev, who has a doctorate from Moscow State University, spoke through a translator. Her speech was more political than Barbara's, focusing on *perestroika* and her hopes for world peace. "In renewing our country, we want to make it open to the world," she said. "The Soviet people know the value of peaceful life. We wish to have good relations with Americans and other people."

The audience also gave Mrs. Gorbachev a standing ovation, and Mrs. Bush embraced her. Both women were mobbed by well-wishers as they made their way out of the tent.

But afterward, many people were struck by the fact that Barbara Bush, emphasizing family values and her personal beliefs, had given a more interesting speech than the highly educated Mrs. Gorbachev, who stuck to the more general themes of *perestroika* and friendship among nations.

TV network commentators and the major newspapers called the day a triumph for Barbara Bush.

"Our First Lady sure beats their First Lady," said *Washington Post* TV critic Tom Shales. "Not that it was a contest of course, but Barbara Bush's speech to graduating seniors at Wellesley College in Massachusetts yesterday, aired on all the networks, was a rock-em-sock-em smash hit, while Raisa Gorbachev's was just your standard graduation address."[9]

The *New York Times* said the speech was "a triumph for

Mrs. Bush, who not only won over most of her audience but to many listeners delivered a more interesting talk than Mrs. Gorbachev, who holds the Soviet equivalent of a Ph.D. and was a university professor before her husband became head of the Soviet communist party."[10]

NBC's Tom Brokaw said on the air that Barbara's talk was "one of the best commencement speeches I've ever heard."

The Wellesley speech seemed to solidify Barbara Bush's popularity. Americans had liked her since her earliest days in the White House. Now she had won new admirers and respect, demonstrating skills and know-how that many Americans hadn't realized she possessed.

"I have never actually had much interest in Barbara Bush, but her refreshing speech at Wellesley College's commencement really impressed me," wrote Rania Nagulb, a student at California State University in a letter to the *Los Angeles Times*. "I would be quite fortunate to follow in her footsteps."[11]

Millions of others felt the same way. By the thousands, they wrote to the White House to express their admiration.

By now Barbara has become accustomed to such accolades, and she has an explanation for the affection she engenders: "I know they find me no threat and they know I care about them—I hope."

If she is sometimes more popular than her husband, a fact she doesn't like to talk about, she has an explanation for that too. "I don't have to make any major decisions. I don't have to take stands on issues I don't want to take them on. I have chosen the cowardly route, which is to pick issues I'm very interested in and work for them."

But Barbara is not known primarily for issues—it's her personality and the style she sets for her family that have captivated Americans.

She is loyal to her husband without being obsequious and stands as a symbol for the millions of women who put home and family first—whether or not they hold jobs in the paid work force. She realizes that many women must work and that others choose to.

"There is a conflict there," she says. "But having said that, it's a fact of life. Our own daughter is going to work full time. She's going to have a struggle. But she's still going to have to sit with her arm around her children and read to them and listen to them and care about them."

Barbara's easy relationship with her five children and twelve grandchildren has delighted a nation that became accustomed over eight years to the sad alienation between Ronald and Nancy Reagan and their children. The Reagan grandchildren were a rare sight at the White House or the Reagans' California ranch. The Bush grandchildren are seen frequently cuddling with their grandparents, both in Washington and at the Bush summer home in Kennebunkport, Maine.

"Barbara Bush is who she is and proud of it and everyone respects that," said Ruth Mandel, director of the Center for the American Woman and Politics at Rutgers University. "She belongs to a class of wives rapidly decreasing in number and unlikely to be seen in the White House in years to come— women who are known as symbols of family life, fulfilled in that role and satisfied with just that."[12]

Despite an upper middle-class childhood, Barbara manages to convey a down-to-earth image, much in contrast to the Park Avenue style Nancy Reagan cultivated.

After the Bushes had been in the White House a little more than a year, the Ikea furniture store, makers of inexpensive do-it-yourself Scandinavian styles, ran an advertisement on the sides of buses in Washington: "Nancy Reagan style at Barbara Bush prices," it said.

Even though she has a grandmotherly image, Barbara does pay attention to her looks and her wardrobe. She has her hair styled regularly and wears designer clothes—Arnold Scaasi and Bill Blass. But since she doesn't dwell on fashion and society—indeed seems to have little interest in them—neither does the nation. She said early on that she was a size 14, had a tendency to gain weight, and wore fake pearls to cover up the wrinkles on her neck. She said she had no plans to dye her white hair or get a face-lift: "I'm so old now that I don't have to pretend to be something I'm not."

During inauguration week in 1989, the Kennedy Center held a salute to the incoming First Lady. She appeared on stage looking great—her hair had been styled, she wore makeup, and her blouse matched the jacket lining of her periwinkle suit.

She turned around slowly, model style, and told the audience, "Please notice: hairdo, makeup, designer dress. Look at me good this week, because it's the only week of my life you're ever going to see it."

When she was invited to speak at the Alfred E. Smith fund-raising dinner in New York in 1989, she used the occasion to poke fun at herself.

"It's not easy being the wife of the president," she said. "Last Sunday a reader of *Parade* magazine wrote in with one of those burning questions. . . . She wrote, 'I would like to know how much Barbara Bush weighs,' " Mrs. Bush said.

"And they answered it. *Parade* magazine says I weigh between 135 and 140 pounds. George said, 'the press never gets anything right.' Just for starters I was born weighing 135 pounds."

Half the women in America identified with this kind of humorous self put-down—"my mail tells me a lot of fat, white-haired, wrinkled ladies are tickled pink"—and Barbara's looks and wardrobe ceased to be a primary topic of conversation.

Since she entered the White House, Mrs. Bush has become more skilled in public speaking, in deflecting questions she doesn't want to answer with less of the sarcasm and prickliness she sometimes exhibited earlier, and in using her popularity and high profile to benefit people and causes that she cares about.

"Aunt Bar, as we call her in the family, is real," said her nephew Jamie Bush. "She's also vulnerable. She speaks from the heart. That's remarkable for someone in politics. Her heart is full of compassion and she speaks with actions as well as words."[13]

During the Persian Gulf war, when the threat of terrorism kept many Americans from flying, Barbara took a commercial jet to visit military families in Indianapolis. She said she wanted to show people that the skies were safe.

Shortly after she became First Lady, she visited Grandma's House, a home for abandoned babies with AIDS. When she picked up one of the infants and cuddled it, the picture ran in newspapers across the country. The message was clear—it's okay to get close to someone with AIDS; the disease isn't easily spread.

The effect on Grandma's House was overwhelming— money and volunteers came pouring in. A later visit to a hospital in New York's Harlem got similar results.

When Washington malls decided to end a longstanding tradition and ban the Salvation Army's bell ringers at Christmas, Barbara made a point of going to a mall, dropping ten dollars into the Salvation Army's bucket, and telling the startled bell ringer, "I'm a great fan of the Salvation Army." Some malls subsequently relented and allowed the bell ringers inside. Barbara said later, "I think I did help the Salvation Army."

Her best-known work has been in literacy. She has had a longtime interest in the subject because one of her four sons, Neil, has dyslexia, a disorder that makes reading difficult. When George Bush was considering a run for the presidency, she decided to give literacy a high profile because she believes that lack of reading skills is the root of many evils.

"Both George and I were brought up to feel that we were very lucky and we ought to give back to society," she said. "And knowing that George was going to run for national office, I spent a whole summer thinking about what would help the most people possible. And it suddenly occurred to me that every single thing I worry about—things like teenage pregnancies, the breakup of families, drugs, AIDS, the homeless—everything would be better if people could read, write, and understand."

Barbara had done a lot of volunteer work before she moved into the White House, and she sought out people whose work she admired and told them so.

In the fall of 1988, shortly after the presidential election, she telephoned Calvin Woodland, who works with troubled youths in Washington. She had read about his work in the newspaper and invited him to lunch to discuss it.

Woodland was surprised to find that he was one of only two guests at the lunch—the other was George Kettle, active in an organization that provides college scholarships to needy students.

Although he had arrived feeling skeptical, Woodland said, he left with a different impression.

"The things we talked about weren't some questions she thought she should ask me because I was a black person," he said. "The lady is the warmest person I've ever met. She had read about the things I had been doing with kids and youth in the community. She told me not to give up, that people do know what is going on and they care about people like me."

The conversation went on for some time, Woodland said, and when Barbara walked her guests to the door, she was still talking. "She gave me a hug and it wasn't a political hug," he said. "It was the kind of hug your mother gives you when you fall down and skin your knee."[14]

It was a typical encounter for Barbara. Her skills at making people feel comfortable are well known, and she and the president clearly enjoy meeting with and entertaining all kinds of people.

Barbara sometimes still appears stiff at large affairs, as if she has mentally withdrawn from the hubbub around her. But that shield fades when she is dealing with people up close—even strangers.

"She looks at you and you feel you've known her for a long time," says Carolyn Pugh, a Republican activist from Columbus, Mississippi. "She's easy to relate to."

Despite all her years in the public eye, Barbara still can get her feelings hurt, especially when criticism is directed at her husband or children—as when the wimp label was put on George Bush during the 1988 campaign, or the savings and loan problem of son Neil. She can be caustic in response, but since an incident in the 1984 presidential campaign when a nasty remark about Democratic vice presidential candidate Geraldine Ferraro made headlines, she has been more cautious.

She doesn't dwell on problems. Her philosophy, she says, is "move on."

And she is always quick to point out that no one should feel sorry for people in public life—least of all her. The rewards far outweigh the drawbacks.

"I feel like I have had the best, the most exciting, thrilling life anyone could ever have," she says. "Imagine knowing heads of every country, on a fairly personal basis in many cases. Or imagine traveling to all those foreign countries. Imagine knowing all the leadership in your own country."

There are the more mundane moments too. Shortly after Barbara moved into the White House, her dog Millie had puppies and she took them for a romp on the South Lawn. They headed for the wrought-iron fence, lined with tourists.

"The most terrible thing happened," she later told reporters. "All five started to wiggle through the fence."

To her relief, the tourists carefully pushed the puppies back inside the White House grounds.

"People were so adorable," she said.

Barbara Bush often exhibits that kind of ease, whether she is entertaining a foreign minister, visiting a group of sick children, or campaigning among common citizens. Her skill with people of all types is what made pundits say before the 1988 election that she would be a First Lady we wouldn't have to train.

The pundits turned out to be right. But Barbara Bush actually had been working on her skills for years, even back in the years when she was still known as Barbara Pierce.

2

Rye Beginnings

*B*arbara Pierce grew up in the comfortable upper middle-class New York City suburbs. She lived in Rye, a fashionable town in Westchester County on Long Island Sound, the third of four children.

June Biedler, a childhood friend of Barbara's, described the suburb this way: "Rye was a small town and although it was certainly a snobby town, it was not one of big estates. People lived in a relatively modest sort of way."

Barbara's father, Marvin, had been a big man on campus at Miami University in Ohio. He was captain of the football team, a top tennis player, and an excellent all-around sportsman. He graduated summa cum laude, then went on to earn degrees in architectural engineering from Harvard and the Massachusetts Institute of Technology.

When Barbara was born—June 8, 1925—Marvin was working his way up the ladder at McCall Publishing Co. Twenty years later, in 1946, he became president of the firm and eventually was named publisher.

Marvin Pierce was a descendant of the fourteenth president of the United States, Franklin Pierce, but Barbara said her family didn't dwell on their famous relation. "The only thing I remember about him was years ago as a child, reading that he was one of our weakest presidents," she said. "I was humiliated."

Marvin's family owned an iron foundry in Sharpsville, Pennsylvania, and had been wealthy. But the year he was born, 1893, coincided with a crash in the iron market, and the family never recovered financially.

Marvin met Pauline Robinson—three years his junior—when she was a student at Oxford College in Ohio. She was a campus beauty and the daughter of an Ohio supreme court justice.

They married in 1918. Their first child, Martha, was born in 1920, and their second, James, nineteen months later. Barbara was the third child, about three and one-half years younger than James. She remained the baby of the family for five years until Scott was born in 1930.

The Pierces lived in a three-story, five-bedroom brick house with a garage, set among large trees on a quarter-acre lot. It was luxurious for the times, but the family of six and their live-in servants—a Chinese husband and wife—filled the space to capacity.

Barbara looked up to her pretty older sister Martha, squabbled with her older brother James, and doted on young Scott, who was in and out of hospitals for years, suffering from a cyst in the bone marrow of his shoulder.

But years later Barbara Bush still can recall how unhappy she was when her mother devoted more attention to her sick son than to her young daughter.

"My mother, I'm sure, was tired and irritable and I didn't understand it at the time," she said. "But I guess I felt neglected that she didn't spend as much time on me. She had this enormous responsibility which I was never sympathetic about. Now, as a mother and grandmother, I realize what she was going through."[1]

Even after Scott recovered, however, Barbara remained much closer to her father than to her mother. She remembers Pauline as a beautiful but humorless woman, a joiner of clubs and a top-notch gardener—she was conservation chairman of the Garden Clubs of America.

Kate Siedle, a childhood friend of Barbara's, recalls Pauline being much involved with her own interests.

"She spent more time in the garden than in the kitchen," Ms. Siedle said. "A lot of the mothers weren't all that motherly, let's put it that way. They had household help and they were social. They had their own little social world."

June Biedler remembered Mrs. Pierce as "very sweet but very austere. One was always scared of her." She fondly recalled, however, that at Barbara's birthday parties, Pauline "would always have either chocolate soufflé or lemon soufflé."

Pauline passed on to Barbara her love of gardening—the hands-on, in-the-dirt type—and also of needlepoint, but Barbara runs a different kind of household. Pauline's house was full of fine antiques and crystal so that "every time you turned around you knocked a piece of Chinese export off the table," Barbara said. Her own homes have always been designed to accommodate the high energy levels of five rambunctious children and now of twelve grandchildren.

Pauline and her daughter also shared a love of dogs. Pauline's dog often had puppies, which were kept in the parental bathroom—a fact that delighted the children, but not the husband.

Barbara had her own dog—Sandy—who appeared with her in a picture that Mrs. Pierce sent to the young George Bush. Barbara Bush's fondness for animals has continued to this day and inspired her to words. When Bush was vice president, she wrote a book about the family's cocker spaniel, *C. Fred's Story*. It sold 15,000 copies, and she donated the proceeds to two national literacy groups, Laubach Literacy Action and Literacy Volunteers of America. When C. Fred died he was replaced by Millie, who went on to become First Dog. Barbara wrote her story as well. *Millie's Book* remained on national best-seller lists for many months.

From her father, Barbara inherited a sense of fun, a sharp wit, and a love of sports. She romped in her brothers' tree house and learned to swim and play competitive tennis at the Manursing Island Club on Long Island Sound.

As she recalls it, her father always took her side, "I think because Mother never took my side." Her girlhood friends remember him being warm and welcoming to children, whereas Pauline Pierce was cold and unapproachable.

Barbara credits her father with the philosophy she used to raise her own children. "He used to say that children should be given lots of love and be shown good examples, in addition to being taught honesty and to follow the work ethic."

Another fond memory was an unusual side benefit from Marvin Pierce's job.

"My dad commuted to New York and he didn't bring his business home with him," Barbara said. "I knew nothing about the publishing business, but I grew up with McCall's pattern books because we waited for the outdated one. He brought it home and we cut out new dolls every year. All my little friends made dresses for them. We'd put them on cardboard and we had our little families and put clothes on them. With that big McCall's pattern book, I was the envy of the neighborhood."[2]

She had several close girlfriends throughout childhood, all about the same age and living within two blocks of one another—June Biedler, Rosanne "Posy" Morgan Clarke, Kate Siedle, Lucille Schoolfield, and Joan Herman. They liked to play make-believe—Lucille enjoyed being Lady Rosanne—and they spent a lot of time playing dress-up in their parents' clothes.

"We acted through the Louisa May Alcott books," said June Biedler, who eventually went on to earn a Ph.D. "And we did a lot of reading." Among their favorites was Hugh Walpole and his "Rogue Harry" series and the love poetry of both Rubert Brooke and Lawrence Hope, a woman who published under a man's name.

"We were around seven" when the poetry reading started,

Dr. Biedler said. "We didn't understand it, but we knew it was a somewhat kind of dirty, adult sort of thing."

But they also climbed trees and played football with the neighborhood boys, and got into "mean" games of croquet. "We played with partners and we had a lot of fun playing it," Ms. Siedle said.

"We were a very close-knit group because we all lived on the same block or parallel streets," Dr. Biedler said. She described Lucille as "the gang leader," a girl who was a year or two older than the others, and who had boy cousins to boot.

It was Lucille who told the others that there was no Santa Claus and, when the time came, about "birds and bees type things."

But it was Barbara who caused mischief among the friends, especially during the fourth and fifth grade. June Biedler and Posy Morgan Clarke both remember the sting when Barbara decided that she and the others would not speak to someone in the group that day.

"She would determine who was speaking to whom when we got on the bus together," Dr. Biedler said. "It would be all planned, nobody's going to talk to June this morning. You'd sit there on the bus with your friends and no one spoke to you. Dreadful feeling."

"She'd call ahead and say, 'We're not going to speak to June this morning,' " Posy Clarke said. "Or she'd call June and say, 'We're not going to speak to Posy.' "

Barbara also zeroed in on weakness. "She could make fun of you and, since I stammered, that was one of her delights," Dr. Biedler said. "She was sort of the leader bully. We were all pretty afraid of her because she could be sarcastic and mean. She was clever, never at a loss for what to say—or what not to say."

Posy Clarke remembered "just absolutely being aghast, 'what have I done?' " when the freeze treatment was turned on her.

"She was a very strong personality as you can plainly see,

and I think she was practicing her skills on us," Ms. Clarke says now.

The hurt from those early humiliations lingered long enough that Dr. Biedler mentioned them to Barbara Bush years later when they had lunch together. "She agreed" that she had been nasty "and she was sweet about it," Dr. Biedler said. Dr. Biedler remains friends with Barbara to this day, as does Posy Clarke.

But the hurt she inflicted on her childhood friends apparently led Barbara to want to make sure there was no repeat in her own household. Her grown children recalled being severely reprimanded if they made fun of someone's weak point—cruel teasing was simply not allowed among the Bush children.

Barbara's girlhood friends all remember her brother James, known to one and all as Jimmy, as a terror. "He was a demon," Ms. Siedle said. "He was sort of the bad boy of the neighborhood. He was a bit wild. He scared us all, he was just that much older."

Once he accidentally shot Barbara in the leg with a BB gun and warned he would kill her if she told their mother. "For a week, I wore high woolen socks and feared death," she said years later.

June Biedler recalled Halloweens where James would ring a doorbell and run "and we would stand there with a raw egg to throw into somebody's house if we didn't like them."

The girls also soaped windows. "That's what we were put up to" by Jimmy and his friends, Dr. Biedler said. "We were glad to have all these boys paying attention to us."

One time, she said, she and Barbara and the others "set fire to the vacant lot next to the Pierces' in order to get the fire company coming," which at the time seemed very exciting. The parents got equally excited, but in a different way, and "We were punished."

The Pierce children did not want for anything, but the family was not as rich as many in the neighborhood. When the girls were older, Lucille Schoolfield bought filet mignon for picnics with her friends and charged it to her parents' account.

Pauline Pierce was something of a spendthrift. Barbara recalls that her mother was always behind on her charge account bills, and after she died in 1949, Marvin was surprised to find that his wife had made deposits on antique furniture at a number of places around the country.

"I mean, she bought on the installment plan all over America," Barbara Bush said disapprovingly. "And nobody dared say, 'Well, Mrs. Pierce never would have done that' because the truth was, she would have."[3]

Barbara was tall as a child and somewhat overweight. At age twelve, she weighed 148 pounds. She remembers family meals fondly.

"We had wonderful food at our house," she said. "We always had real cream on our cereal and mashed potatoes made from the real McCoy." Posy Clarke recalls walking back and forth for lunch with Barbara to the Rye Country Day School in the junior high years, eating jelly rolls along the way.

Although Barbara wasn't concerned about her weight, her mother was. "I spent all my life with my mother saying 'Eat up, Martha' to my older sister and 'Not you, Barbara.' "

She attended dancing class on Friday nights and found that boys—often not as tall as she—chose shorter girls as partners. So Barbara danced with her girlfriends, usually taking the part of the boy.

"I didn't want to be left. Not me. I was five feet eight at the age of twelve."

The dancing lessons were formal. Both boys and girls wore white gloves. Boys bowed when they asked a girl to dance.

"Miss Covington [the dance instructor] was a rather large-bosomed lady who would wear black lace and glide up the floor," demonstrating with the "lead foot" and the "copy-cat" foot, Kate Siedle recalled.

"We were told never to put our weight on the arms of the

boy," she said. "The elbow was to be pointing out so you didn't make the job too hard for him. It wasn't the jitterbug or anything. It was the waltz and the fox-trot. When we left, we curtsied and shook hands with Miss Covington. This was in the Episcopal Church."

The dancing lessons were put to good use later at country club parties arranged by parents. Millie Dent, who grew up in the area at the same time Barbara Pierce did, recalled that mothers "worked like dogs to get extra boys" so that girls would not be left standing on the sidelines.

During the teen years, "No girls danced with girls," she said. "You'd rather be caught dead."

At the beginning of a dance, Mrs. Dent said, a large crowd of boys would gather on one side of the room in a stag line. When one of them spotted an attractive girl, he would ask her to dance. But first he would arrange for several buddies to cut in on him. That way he wouldn't get "stuck" if he didn't like the girl.

This arrangement also worked wonderfully for the girls because they were always getting new partners—even if not for the reasons they might have wished. "You felt popular whether you were or not," Mrs. Dent said. "We felt like we were butterflies. It was fun. You met a lot of people that way. It was just a wonderful solution."

But Barbara's friends said she never had to worry about standing on the sidelines by the time she was a teen.

Even though she had been plumpish as a child, "she became so pretty, the boys were wild about her," June Biedler said.

"She had more beaus than anybody," Posy Clarke said. "She was just extremely popular. She was just awfully good with people. She was like her father, who was a delightful man. She was confident, very confident."

Mrs. Dent was friendly with Barbara's brother James at the time, and years later in Washington became a friend of Barbara Bush's. She recalled the Pierce family as a standout because the four children had a friendly, welcoming manner about them.

As a young girl, Mrs. Dent spent summers in Bedford Hills, a neighboring suburb of Rye. Since Manursing was the nearest country club, she and her friends were taken there by their parents to swim and play tennis.

Coming from another town, they felt unsure of themselves at first, but soon found that "there were about three big families that were a lot of fun [one of them the Pierces]. They were outgoing, that was the thing," Mrs. Dent said. "We were sort of shy and they just made us feel at home and we enjoyed them."

Barbara went to the local public school through the sixth grade. She still recalls, with mixed feelings, her first day there.

"At age six, in 1931, my mother led me by the hand into the public school at Rye, New York," she said. "We met the teacher and then my mother was gone. She disappeared with no good-byes. I felt abandoned. But I truly loved school so much I forgave her by the time I got home."

Along with most of her friends, Barbara transferred to the private Rye Country Day School after elementary school. For her junior and senior years, she was sent away to a finishing school—Ashley Hall in Charleston, South Carolina—just as her sister Martha had been.

"My mother thought my sister and I should be exposed to different areas of the country," Barbara said. "She thought we should be exposed to the South."

June Biedler said many students went away for junior and senior year because the Rye school "was just not that good. And in those days, in some cases, those schools [out of town] were meant to be sort of finishing up. But in any case, the schools were good—high educational standards."

By the time Martha graduated from Ashley Hall, she had become a beauty, just like her mother. In August 1940, while she was at Smith College, Martha was chosen for the cover of a college issue of *Vogue* magazine. She was posed in an above-the-knee skirt with shirt and blazer, loafers and bobby socks—and leg warmers. An antique big-wheeled bicycle was used as the backdrop.

Friends from both Rye and Ashley Hall describe Martha as a knockout and Barbara as quite pretty.

But when she gathered with future classmates at New York City's Grand Central Station for the trip south in September 1941, Barbara's self-image was low.

"There were a lot of fat squatty girls there, leaving for Ashley Hall," she said years later. "I felt miserable."

All through the trip, Barbara thought about the friends and good times she was leaving behind. Her mood had not improved by the time she reached Charleston.

"I distinctly remember walking up the long flight of stairs to the third floor," she said. "I felt miserable for about four minutes—until I got to know some other girls."[4]

During her junior year, Barbara Pierce shared a room with three classmates. "The room was very ample," said roommate Cordelia Lambert Stites. "We had a fireplace and nice big windows looking out over the oak, dripping with Spanish moss."

The closets and the community bath were in the hall, leaving plenty of space in the room for sprawling, studying, and daydreaming.

Ashley Hall had only 150 students at the time. The education was classical and the atmosphere proper and straightlaced.

"Boarding students like Barbara Pierce couldn't go outside the school unless they were wearing a hat, gloves, and no lipstick," said Jane Lucas Thornhill, a classmate at the time. "Anyone could recognize a group of Ashley girls coming down the street a block away."

Classmate Miriam House, who lived in Charleston, recalled arriving at school one Monday morning with her nail polish still on. "I had to go into the library and have it removed," she said.

Barbara herself recalls being confined to campus most of the time. "We hardly went out at all," she said. "It was right in the middle of the war and the navy men were in town. I don't think it was until my senior year that we could go to church on Sunday without a chaperone."

On mixed social occasions, the chaperones were especially vigilant. Barbara remembers attending a dance at The Citadel, a military academy in Charleston, and being accompanied by an attentive chaperone: "That lady never let me out of her sight."

Mrs. Thornhill, who lived in Charleston, said she frequently invited classmates to her home—her mother had to sign them out—and they were eager to come "because they wanted to see boys."

But she said Barbara—called "Barbi" by her classmates—"didn't go out as much as the others and wasn't really looking around at the Charleston boys."

Mrs. Stites said Barbara did have several casual dates with a young man at The Citadel who had gone out with her older sister Martha earlier.

While there were no serious romances, Barbara and Cordelia worked together to thwart one especially onerous rule at Ashley Hall.

Girls were allowed to invite dates into the parlor for two hours on Sunday afternoons—with no chaperone in the room. "But you couldn't have the same boy two weekends in a row. So Barbara and I traded off a couple of times," each one signing up for the other one's date.

Another roommate, Susan Estey Edgerly, was president of the student government at Ashley Hall and got the best grades in the class. She remembers Barbara Pierce as attractive and self-confident.

"She was just the prettiest thing and very outgoing and athletic at Ashley Hall," Mrs. Edgerly said. "I envied her. She was slender and I was fat. In recent years, I've gotten slender and she's gotten a little heavier"—a fact she and Barbara laughed over the last time they saw one another.

Despite all the restrictions at Ashley Hall, Barbara was happy at the school. She even has fond memories of the headmistress, Mary Vardrine McBee.

"I remember her as rather short and round," she said. "I rather liked her, which wasn't a very popular thing to do."

The educational program was rigorous, and Barbara was a good student. "She loved history and English and she was quite good in French," Mrs. Stites said.

There were two study halls every day—one in the afternoon and one in the evening—both monitored by teachers. And when the girls weren't studying, they were kept busy with sports and extracurricular activities. Barbara was a member of both the student council and drama club, and she kept up her swimming and tennis.

As a junior, she played Beatrice in the Shakespearean comedy *Much Ado About Nothing*. During her senior year, she and Cordelia Lambert played the twin roles in *Twelfth Night*.

"During one of my two years, I was an angel with a speaking role in the Christmas play," Barbara recalled. "And—I think I'm right—I was the underwater swimming champion of the Class of '43. I swam something like two and one-half times across the pool."

The girls at Ashley Hall were acutely aware of the war. The dining room was sandbagged and used as an air raid shelter as well as for meals. And the Class of 1943 decided to give up its yearbook to help the troops.

"That was the only year Ashley Hall didn't have an annual," said classmate Frances Baker Turnage. "It was during the war, and we contributed the paper to the cause. Instead, we exchanged pictures."

Mrs. Turnage said that Barbara wrote on the back of hers, "Please let me know when something important happens to you. I know I'll hear from you first. Love, Barbi."

Barbara wrote that affectionate message even though she and Frances were not close friends—Frances was a day student and Barbara a boarder.

"We knew each other mostly in sports and classroom activities," Mrs. Turnage said. "I remember her being quiet and ladylike—not loud. A good girl."

Other classmates and teachers must have agreed with that assessment. When she graduated, Barbara was awarded the Rosalie McCabe Cup for general sportsmanship at Ashley Hall.

Barbara has kept in contact with Ashley Hall and some of her classmates over the years. For the fortieth reunion of the Class of '43, she invited all members to Washington. And during the years the Bushes lived in the vice presidential mansion in Washington, several groups of young Ashley Hall students were taken on special tours.

Despite all the fun she had at Ashley Hall, Barbara Pierce retained strong social ties to her friends back home. It was during an outing with them—over the Christmas holidays of her junior year—that she came upon a real romance.

"I Could Hardly Breathe When He Was in the Room"

Geeorge Bush was rich, smart, friendly, and a big man on campus. But none of those qualities comes to mind when Barbara Bush recalls what first attracted her.

"He was the handsomest-looking man you ever laid your eyes on, bar none," she says. "I mean, my boys don't even come close to him, nor did his own brothers."

They met at a dance at the Round Hill Country Club in Greenwich, Connecticut, during Christmas vacation in 1941. In his autobiography, *Looking Forward,* George Bush remembered the occasion in detail:

"I'm not much at recalling what people wear, but that particular occasion stands out in my memory," he said. "The band was playing Glenn Miller tunes when I approached a friend from Rye, New York, Jack Wozencraft, to ask if he knew a girl across the dance floor, the one wearing the green and red holiday dress.

"He said she was Barbara Pierce, that she lived in Rye and

went to school in South Carolina. Would I like an introduction? I told him that was the general idea and he introduced us just about the time the bandleader decided to change tempos, from fox-trot to waltz. Since I didn't waltz, we sat the dance out. And several more after that, talking and getting to know each other."[1]

Barbara recalls the evening more romantically. She was so taken with this good-looking, self-assured, outgoing boy that "I could hardly breathe when he was in the room."

The Bushes have obviously repeated this story fondly for their children, each of whom adds his own spin.

"It seems that my dad was zonked over the head by this outgoing, charming woman," says number-four son Marvin. "And just like everything else he's done in his life, he decided that she was the one he was going to marry and so he did."

"I'm told it was love at first sight," said number-one son George. "I think Mother had heard of George Bush's reputation from a nearby city and Dad saw Mother at a party and fell in love with her."

George Bush, known as Poppy during his childhood and teen years, grew up in Greenwich, Connecticut, an upper-class New York City suburb. His family had a lot of money—even during the Great Depression there were three full-time maids and a chauffeur who took the Bush boys to the Greenwich Country Day School.

But Prescott and Dorothy Bush hewed to the Puritan ethic. They believed in hard work, temperate living, and daily Bible readings. Prescott was not averse to using a belt for discipline, and the boys were required to wear jackets and ties at dinner and to speak at the dinner table only when spoken to.

Prescott Bush was a Wall Street investment banker, a graduate of Phillips Academy in Andover, Massachusetts, and of Yale. He was a strict man who expected a lot of his children, and young George was much in awe of him. He still recalls his father with great respect, but also as "pretty scary."

George's mother, Dorothy Walker Bush, was more fun.

She had a cheerful personality and, like her husband, a love of competitive sports—they got all the children involved in them. Her father, George Herbert Walker, had been a highly successful investor with a strong interest in golf—he donated money for the Walker Cup that still bears his name. George Walker also built the family summer house at Kennebunkport, Maine, that George and Barbara Bush now use as a favorite retreat.

The Bush children spent their spare time playing tennis, golf, baseball, and card games. They swam and hunted and learned early that trying hard to win was important. Bush has recalled returning home from tennis when he was about eight years old and telling his mother he had been off his game.

"You don't have a game," she replied. "Get out and work harder and maybe someday you will."

But the Bush children were close, especially Prescott Junior and George, the first two sons born just twenty-one months apart. Dorothy Bush remembers giving the two separate rooms for the first time when the family moved into a larger house. A psychologist she heard at a lecture had recommended such a move.

"So we put Pres and George each in his own room," Mrs. Bush said. "That was in September. Then along in November the two boys came to their father and me and said, 'Do you know what we want for Christmas? It won't cost you anything but we would like to tell you now.' What they wanted was to go back to sharing the same room. And that's the way it was until they grew up and left home to get married."

George started school a year early so he could be with Prescott during the day instead of being left home without a playmate. That meant he was a year ahead when he entered prep school at Andover, which was fortunate because he developed a respiratory infection during his junior year that put him behind in his studies. Between his early entry and his illness, he spent five years at the school, graduating in 1942.

George was a senior at Andover when he went home for Christmas in 1941. It was a busy social season, and the dance at the Round Hill Club was one of several that teens in the area attended during the holidays. They were formal affairs—boys in tuxedos and girls in long dresses. An orchestra provided live music, the punch was alcohol-free, and there were plenty of chaperones.

After George and Barbara were introduced, they sat and talked through several dances, then each returned home with friends, George to Greenwich, Barbara to Rye. Barbara told her mother that night she had met someone she liked. By the time she woke up the next morning—late—her mother had already been on the telephone investigating.

Barbara was miffed, but the thought of the handsome young man from Greenwich soon took the edge off her anger. That night they saw one another again at a dance at the Apawamis Club in Rye.

This time George cut in on Barbara and asked her for a date. Just at that moment, however, Barbara's brother James cut in on George. His purpose was to get his sister out of the way so he could convince George to take part in a basketball competition.

George figured out a way to please both of the young Pierces—he agreed to play in the game, set for a few days later, and he asked if Barbara would be there and whether he could drive her home. The date was set.

Barbara, who had shown scant interest in basketball to that point, suggested her whole family go to watch James play in the upcoming game. And everyone went along with her plan—they all wanted to take a look at the boy who had captured her attention.

George borrowed the family car, thankful that it had a radio in case long silences developed during the date. As it turned out, he needn't have worried. He and Barbara went out for ice cream sodas and found themselves in easy conversation.

When Christmas vacation was over, George returned to

Andover and Barbara to Ashley Hall. They were bursting with excitement about one other.

"She came back from vacation full of news about a new boyfriend by the name of Poppy Bush," Susan Edgerly recalls. "She was pretty much in love, I guess, and then he started writing and she shared his love letters with us. He was certainly wooing her."

Although the girls shared their letters, they read only parts to their roommates and the letters never actually changed hands.

Mrs. Edgerly said Barbara Pierce "was a kind of shy person in the love department, and I can remember her shyness and kind of almost blushing when she read those letters. She would be almost embarrassed but loved every word of it."

The fourth roommate, Shavaun Robinson Towers, had a mailbox right next to Barbara's and remembered with amusement how she kept a close and jealous eye on the Pierce mail.

"She got a letter from George Bush every damned day, and once a week I got a letter from my mother," Mrs. Towers said.

When Barbara met George she already had a boyfriend—a nuzzling, nonkissing relationship, as she describes it—but quickly lost all interest in him. It was, she said, a fortunate turn of events.

"I had a beau at the time and to show how lucky life can be, he now has had four wives," she said. "It's true and all twenty years younger. I would have been gone long ago."

As it was, George banished all thoughts of her earlier puppy-love relationship. In her spare time, "she used to knit argyle socks for George," Cordelia Stites said.

George and Barbara saw each other again at spring break on the single day that their vacations overlapped. They went on a double date to see *Citizen Kane*. Afterward, George walked Barbara to the door and kissed her good night. It was the spring of 1942 and she was almost seventeen years old. He was the first boy she had ever kissed.

Once again Barbara returned to school talking about Poppy and full of plans for the future.

"He had asked her to crew on one of the races on his sailboat and she was very excited about that," Cordelia Stites said.

At the end of the school year, George invited Barbara to his senior prom, held in the school gymnasium.

Their romance developed more fully during the summer that followed, but the shadow of war loomed large over their plans. George had decided right after the Japanese bombed Pearl Harbor—December 1941, the same month he met Barbara—that he would not go straight on to Yale after graduation, even though he had been accepted. He wanted to join the navy and take part in the war.

So in June of 1942, as soon as he turned eighteen, George Bush signed up as a seaman second class. Two months later, on August 6, he reported for duty at the navy's preflight training center in Chapel Hill, North Carolina. He took a train from New York City, feeling frightened and alone, much as Barbara had a year earlier when she made her first journey to Ashley Hall.

But just as she quickly learned to fit in with her schoolmates, George made friends at Chapel Hill. As the youngest in the group of trainees, however, he was conscious of both his age and a face that made him look even younger. He had been in training only a few weeks when Barbara wrote to say she planned to stop by and see him on her way back to Ashley Hall for the start of senior year. When he met her at the train station, the self-conscious Bush asked her to tell everyone that she was eighteen, even though she had just turned seventeen a few months earlier.

They held hands as they walked around the grounds, and George introduced Barbara to his friends. And, of course, she said, not a soul asked how old she was.

During her senior year, Barbara saw little of her boyfriend, but they kept in close touch by letter. "She was a one-man woman as I recall and writing letters constantly, not like the telephoning that young people do today," said Marjorie Macnutt Thurstone, Barbara's lone roommate during senior year.

Mrs. Thurstone said she and Barbara were both active in student government and "we became good friends. . . . We'd sit in our room and talk." She also remembered Barbara as a good student during her final year in high school— "I think we both studied hard. Her getting into Smith proved that."

Meanwhile, George finished his initial training at Chapel Hill, got further training in Minneapolis from November to February, and completed the ten-month basic flight-training course at Corpus Christi, Texas, in June. He received his ensign's bars on June 9, 1943, and was exultant at becoming a real navy pilot.

Barbara graduated from high school that same month along with her twenty-nine classmates. When she returned to Ashley Hall forty-one years later as commencement speaker, she thanked the school for "allowing me to relive some of the happiest days of my life."[2]

She spent the summer at home in Rye, thinking about George Bush but also preparing for college. She had been accepted at Smith, just as her sister Martha had been a couple of years earlier. A number of her classmates from Ashley Hall also were going there. Roommate Susan Edgerly said her mother sent her to Ashley Hall upon the recommendation of a Smith counselor, who said if Susan wanted to get into Smith, Ashley Hall was the best preparation she would find. Barbara's brother James also went to a top school, Bowdoin in Brunswick, Maine. Scott graduated from his parents' alma mater, Miami University in Ohio.

George spent most of the summer in advanced flight training, learning to land on an aircraft carrier, but in August he had time off and invited Barbara to Kennebunkport to stay with his family.

It was an idyllic seventeen-day vacation for the young couple—the last extended time they would have together for a while. They sailed, played tennis, rode bicycles, went on picnics, hung around with the large Bush family—and decided they would get married.

Barbara said George never formally proposed to her on bended knee or otherwise. They just talked about their future together and decided to become engaged. They told their families but decided not to make a formal announcement until the following December.

Although Barbara was just eighteen and George nineteen and neither had yet spent a day in college, their parents did not object to the engagement. Barbara said her parents had put up a fight a short time earlier when her sister Martha married a Yale senior and they weren't ready for another battle.

"Also, there was a war going on," she said. "One has to remember that when you got engaged at that time you weren't sure you would ever see that person again when they went overseas. I know my mother and father really liked George but I don't think they believed we would get married. I believe they were thinking they would take it one step at a time. George's parents probably felt the same way."[3]

At the end of the summer, George reported for duty at the naval air base at Norfolk, Virginia, and joined a new squadron that was assigned to Chincoteague, a peninsula in Virginia, for his final training.

Barbara began her freshman year at Smith College in Northampton, Massachusetts. She had to make new friends in college because Smith had a policy of assigning girls from each prep school to different living quarters. That wasn't a problem for Barbara, who socialized easily.

In fact, she spent much more time having fun, writing to George, and playing sports than studying. Her grades suffered.

"I didn't like to study very much," she said in 1988 when the controversy over Dan Quayle's college records erupted. "I'd hate to have anybody go through my records from freshman year. I was all right in high school, but when it came to

Smith, I was a cliffhanger. The truth is, I just wasn't very interested. I was just interested in George."

She was active on campus, however. Always athletic, she was named captain of her eleven-member interclass soccer team, playing the position of center half.[4] She also played lacrosse, went to the movies on Saturday night, and kept her spirits up, if not her grades.

Her father sent her copies of *McCall's* magazine each month, much to the displeasure of the Smith administrators.

"One day they came to me and they said, 'We notice you're getting pulp magazines in the mail. We don't allow pulp magazines,'" Mrs. Bush recalled. "I phoned my dad and said, 'Dad, I can't get those magazines. They're pulp magazines.' He said, 'You tell that lady you're getting those magazines and you wouldn't be there if it wasn't for pulp magazines.'"

The high point of the year came in December when George was in Philadelphia to attend a commissioning ceremony for the USS *San Jacinto,* a new carrier that was to become home to his squadron. He invited Barbara and his mother Dorothy to attend the festivities. The two women traveled to Philadelphia together on the train.

Barbara was nervous being alone with George's mother, but she was savvy enough to hold her tongue when the question of an engagement ring came up.

Dorothy Bush asked what kind of ring Barbara wanted. Barbara said she didn't care. "Does it have to be a diamond?" Dorothy asked. Again Barbara said she didn't care, unaware that Mrs. Bush was carrying in her purse a star sapphire ring that had belonged to George's aunt, Nancy Walker.

"Just before the commissioning ceremony started, George took the ring out of his pocket and gave it to me," Barbara said. "I was thrilled. I don't know to this day whether it's real and I don't care. It's my engagement ring and it hasn't been off my finger since the day George gave it to me."[5]

Three months later, in March 1944, George shipped out

with his squadron for the South Pacific. Barbara finished her freshman year at Smith and wrote a lot of letters.

That fall she returned to school but soon dropped out. Her head was full of wedding plans, and the thought of more Latin, history, and English left her cold. She and George planned to be married on December 19 and she had a lot to do. It was the end of her formal education.

"I took a leave of absence from Smith to be married and never went back," she said later. "In those days there were not many coeducational colleges, and when George got out of the navy he went to Yale. I have to be absolutely frank. I could have gone to Connecticut College [near Yale] and George Bush would have killed himself to have gotten me there [to get her degree]. If you want to do anything in life, you can do it. But the truth is, I didn't want to do it. Now I am sorry I don't have that in my background."

George began flying missions against the Japanese in May 1944 and had a number of harrowing experiences in the air during the summer.

On September 2 his plane was hit by antiaircraft fire while he was on a bombing mission against one of the Bonin Islands, Chichi Jima. He bailed out and, with help from a buddy in another plane, spotted his raft about fifty feet away. He was in the water for almost three hours before being rescued by a submarine. He remained on the craft for thirty days, out of touch with the world. When he was finally put ashore and flown to Pearl Harbor, he immediately sent a telegram to his parents.

The senior Bushes had been told by one of George's friends that he was missing, but they kept the news from Barbara as long as they could.

She had begun to worry anyway, however, because she hadn't received a letter from him in a long time. When Dorothy Bush phoned to tell her of the telegram, Barbara cried with joy.

George arrived home from the war on Christmas Eve,

1944. In his autobiography, he described the scene like something out of the movies—a holiday setting, kisses, hugs, joy, and laughter. He was home, his fiancée by his side, his family all around him.

He had missed his wedding day, but that was no problem. Barbara was happy to reschedule. George and Barbara were married on January 6, 1945, nineteen days later than planned.

Barbara wore a long-sleeved white satin dress and a veil that had belonged to her mother-in-law. George was in his navy dress blues. The eight bridesmaids, including Ashley Hall roommate Shavaun Robinson Towers and childhood friend Posy Morgan Clarke, wore cap-sleeved, high-necked emerald green satin dresses "with green ostrich feathers that curled around in our hair," Mrs. Clarke said. They carried red and white carnations. George's older brother Prescott, who had himself married just a week earlier, interrupted his honeymoon to be best man. But most of the ushers, Mrs. Towers said, were "whoever was around" because so many of George's friends were fighting in the war.

"The wedding was lovely," Mrs. Clarke said. "The night before, there was a dinner in Greenwich, given by the groom's parents."

She said Barbara later gave each of the bridesmaids a framed picture of the wedding party.

The reception, for more than 250 guests, was at the Apawamis Club in Rye, where George and Barbara had made their first date. The bride and groom led off the dancing, much to George's displeasure. He whispered to his bride, "I hope you're having a good time. Enjoy it. It's the last time I'll ever dance in public."

For their honeymoon, the young couple set off in high spirits for a resort on Sea Island, Georgia. It was all too short, however. George was still in the navy and in line for special training that would prepare him to take part in a final assault on Japan planned for later in the year. The young husband moved with his group from Florida to Michigan to Maine and then to Oceana Naval Air Station in Virginia. Barbara joined him when she could. In their one-room apartment in Wyandotte, Michigan, she discovered that she had much to learn as a housekeeper. "I ruined everything—and I mean everything," she said. "I shrank my whole trousseau. That was a weakness of my mother. She had a theory that if you could read, you could keep house."

George and Barbara were together in Virginia Beach by August that year when news came that Japan had surrendered. On August 14 they listened to a radio broadcast of President Truman's speech: "I have received this afternoon a message from the Japanese government in reply to the message forwarded to that government by the secretary of state on August 11. I deem this reply a full acceptance of the Potsdam Declaration, which specifies the unconditional surrender of Japan."

The Bushes, like all the young couples on base and elsewhere, were overjoyed. The end of the war meant they would lose no more friends in combat and that George would not have to ship out for a final assault on Japan.

In Virginia Beach, the streets quickly filled with celebrants. The Bushes joined their friends for the festivities—but only after going to church to thank God that the war was at an end.

Because he had been in combat and received decorations, George was able to get a discharge from the navy just a month after the war ended. Two months later he was enrolled at Yale under a special program for veterans that would allow them to graduate in two and one-half years. Five thousand of the eight thousand Yale freshmen that year were returning servicemen.

Housing was in short supply but George and Barbara managed to get an apartment on Whitney Avenue in New Haven, not far from campus. The apartment was one of thirteen carved out of an old house, and it soon got a little more crowded—the Bushes' first child, George, was born July 6,

1946, in the first year of the Baby Boom. Not to worry, though. All the other apartments in the building also were filled with young couples, and each had a child.

The Bushes had their own bathroom, but they shared a kitchen with two other families. It had two stoves, two refrigerators, and orange crates on the wall that served as cabinets. Each family cooked in the kitchen, then used a tea cart to wheel the food back to the apartment. "There wasn't any fancy system and there wasn't any problem with schedules," said one of the neighbors. "It was great fun. It was a wonderful way to start. Everybody was sort of in the same boat."

Even though the apartment was small, George and Barbara entertained frequently. Their nearby relatives often came for visits, along with friends. Barbara, already developing her excellent organizational skills, learned to cook foods that could be made ahead of time.

George majored in economics and minored in sociology. He studied hard enough to earn Phi Beta Kappa, an academic honor, but he also played baseball enthusiastically, becoming team captain by his senior year. His first spring at Yale he played first base. Barbara, pregnant with young George, kept score and did it well, a fact that George remarked on proudly years later: "Not many people know how to score a baseball game."

Money was tight for everyone, including the Bushes. Before the baby came, Barbara worked at the Yale Coop to help bolster the family finances. (The family lived on money George had saved during the war from his military paycheck.)

Like other young couples, the Bushes also were planning for the future. Bush, in his autobiography, said that after reading *The Farm* by Louis Bromfield, he and Barbara imagined themselves settling in the Midwest and raising a family among wide pastures and fields of grain. But when they looked into the costs, they realized they didn't have enough money to get started.

"If I'd really believed there was a solid business prospect to discuss, I wouldn't have hesitated to go to Dad," Bush said. "No matter how we looked at it though, George and Barbara Farms came off as a high-risk, no-yield investment."[6]

What the Bushes finally settled on was just as exotic as farming. A friend of the senior Bushes, Neil Mallon, suggested the young couple head for Texas to learn the oil business. Mallon, an oilman himself, was head of Dresser Industries, and he offered George a job at the International Derrick and Equipment Co.—Ideco—one of Dresser's subsidiaries. George would start as an equipment clerk.

He had saved $3,000 from his navy pay, and his father gave him a 1947 red Studebaker when he graduated from Yale. It was all the young couple needed to start life in a different—very different—part of the country.

George was raring to go, having gotten a taste of the wider world outside Greenwich while he was in the navy. He wanted to be out from under his father's shadow so he could make his own mark in the world.

Barbara, however, had assumed that she and George would settle in familiar New England. She reacted to the idea of venturing to the wilds of Texas with a baby the same way she had initially viewed enrollment in Ashley Hall—with fear. But characteristically, she accepted with good humor the hand that fate had dealt her.

"I didn't want to go at the time," she said. "But a day after I got there, I thought it was really exciting. . . . If we had been bound by our past, we'd have stayed in Greenwich or Rye and done our thing like everybody else in our family did. But we ventured out."

Also, she said, "I've been brought up in a family where if your husband wanted to do something, you'd do it, and gladly. I still think there's nothing really wrong with that. I would say the same if a wife wanted to do something very badly. Her husband should do the same."

In later years, Barbara realized that the shock of the move west took her out of the cocoon she had been in since childhood and helped her mature much more quickly.

"I remember I never bought a thing by myself," she said. "My mother and my sister bought everything and told me, 'This would be nice for you.' And after I was married . . . I went off and bought a tweed suit, brought it home to show my mother and Mrs. Bush, my first purchase. And they both said, 'Well, no hem, dear, and the color—so drab.' And whatever. 'It's cheap, dear.' Well, I think I kept it and hated it from then on . . . I really was a late bloomer, in all honesty."[7]

Right after graduation from Yale, George took the Studebaker and drove cross country to find a place for his young family to settle. Barbara and young George followed a week later by plane—a propeller flight of more than twelve hours. It was the start of a big adventure.

Texas

George and Barbara were both accustomed to large, comfortable homes, household help, lush green surroundings, and friends and neighbors schooled in upper-class traditions. Life in Texas would be completely different.

George's first job was in Odessa, a strictly utilitarian town carved out of the harsh West Texas sagebrush. Its main business was oil, and no attempt had been made to beautify the surroundings. The town consisted mostly of equipment yards.

George found a house on East Seventh Street, divided into two apartments. The Bushes had their own kitchen, a living room, and one bedroom with a rattling window fan. They shared a bath with the other tenants—a mother-and-daughter prostitution team—and the women's many guests.

"Everything in life is relative," Barbara said. "We had the only house on the street with a bathroom and the only car."

Despite their odd surroundings, the young couple experienced a sense of exhilaration being on their own, far away from their powerful families.

"It was the first time in our lives that we had lived in a place where nobody said, 'You're Marvin Pierce's daughter or Pres Bush's son,' " Barbara said. "It's pretty nice to be judged on your own."

Although they had little money, they had confidence in George's earning power, knew that family money would be available in an emergency, and never considered themselves poor.

"We both knew that if we got into trouble someone would help us," Barbara said. "And so to say we knew what it was like to be poor is ridiculous. For us, it was a challenge and exciting and we'd rather have died than asked. But it's very easy to say when you know you've got a mother and father—in fact, two—who would help . . . that's very different."

Still, Barbara recalls with amusement that her mother used to send her Ivory soap, imagining that it wasn't available in the Wild West, and "we were so poor, I let her."

But there was no help available from home in learning the cultural mores of West Texas. The white-gloves lessons of Ashley Hall and Smith and the bonhomie of Yale didn't apply there.

"George wore Bermuda shorts one day and got whistled off the street," Barbara said. "He came home so quickly you couldn't see him for the dust."

Neither of the Bushes were big drinkers, but they kept one bottle of liquor for special occasions and guests.

"We had one bottle, which was ruined for us the first time a man walked through the door," Barbara said. "George offered him a drink, and he took our one bottle—and drank out of it."

George also had his first experience getting dead drunk—on Christmas Eve, 1948, just months after he and Barbara had arrived. As he tells the story in his autobiography, he was a co-host at Ideco's office Christmas party, held right in the company's supply store. Barbara and little George were waiting at home for him so they could decorate the tree together. But as the evening progressed, more and more guests came to the party and George kept filling

drinks—and taking one for himself. He said he doesn't remember when the party ended, but Barbara tells him that a
colleague eventually put him in the back of a pickup truck
and took him home, depositing him gently on the front
lawn.

Early on, the Bushes learned how much sports meant in
Texas.

"I had played baseball and soccer in college and knew how
intense athletic competition can get," George said. "But Barbara and I had never experienced anything like the fever that
took over Odessa during the football season. It was more
than a game. It was a total experience. There were overflow
crowds on Friday nights for high school games and whole
towns would travel by caravan to neighboring towns to settle bragging rights for the coming year . . .

"All this was different for Barbara and me. Like millions
who had come West to start new lives before us, and like
millions who have come since, we had a lot to learn about the
customs of our new home. But learn we did, because that,
when you get right down to it, was what we had come to
Texas to do—to shape our own lives and bring up our kids
in a land of fresh challenge and opportunity."[1]

The Bushes lived in Odessa less than a year. Dresser Industries had better things in mind for George, and he was
transferred to California, where he became a full-fledged
salesman. The downside was that the family of three had to
move five times in a single year—from Huntington Park to
Bakersfield to Whittier to Ventura to Compton—and George
traveled one thousand miles a week.

When their second child, Pauline Robinson Bush, was
born in Compton in December 1949, Barbara met her doctor
the day the baby was delivered. The Bushes had been in
town such a short time they hardly had time to get to know
their neighbors, much less develop the usual wider community contacts.

The baby was named after Barbara's mother, Pauline, who
had been killed in a freak car accident just two months ear-

lier. Pauline had set a hot cup of coffee on the car seat next to her one morning while riding with her husband. Marvin saw the cup starting to slide toward her and reached over to get it. He lost control of the car on one of Westchester County's narrow country lanes and crashed into a stone wall. Pauline was killed instantly.

Barbara, seven months pregnant, did not go to the funeral. Her father, who suffered several broken ribs in the accident, urged her not to, fearing that the cross-country trip would be bad for the baby. Barbara agreed, but she later came to regret the decision.

"I'll never forgive myself for not going to my mother's funeral or spending time with my father in the hospital," she says now.[2]

Shortly after their daughter was born, the Bushes moved back to Texas. This time Dresser Industries sent them to Midland, another scrub town but one filled with ambitious young couples from other places, families just like themselves, raising children and trying to make a killing in the oil business.

The Bushes bought a house for $7,500—847 square feet. It was part of a development, the first of its kind in Midland, and had a floor plan identical to all the other houses in the neighborhood. To compensate for this, the developer had painted each house a different pastel color. The area became known as Easter Egg Row.

Barbara and George settled into the neighborhood comfortably, finding many kindred souls. All the women spent their days tending young children—three, four, and five children per family. The men worked long hours, many of them in the oilfield, checking out prospects and problems.

"It was just the right time to live there," Barbara said. "I remember Dad visiting us in Midland and saying, 'I worry about you. What if something happened? Who would support you?' Well, we were all in the same situation. No one had any family. We were all newcomers and we came from all over the country. We formed really good friendships."[3]

Because Midland lacked cultural amenities, the young families had to make their own fun. Backyard barbecues—held after church on Sundays—were generally the week's big event. If there were enough people, a softball game might develop. It was all friendly and very informal.

Martin Allday, a Midland lawyer, recalls the days when he was courting the girl he would later marry. She lived near the Bushes. One day, he said, "I went over to pick her up and Bush and Barbara and the kids came walking across the street barefooted, sat down in the backyard to have a beer with my father-in-law."[4]

Bush had not been in Midland long before he decided to leave Dresser Industries and start his own oil firm. He went into business with one of his neighbors, John Overbey, who was already an independent operator, trading in oil leases and mineral rights. In late 1950 they formed the Bush-Overbey Oil Development Co., with financial help from Bush's uncle, Herbert Walker. Bush was twenty-six years old.

The company was profitable from the start. Bush was able to use his impressive contacts back East to raise the money needed to buy mineral rights and arrange for oil exploration. One of his investors was Eugene Meyer, owner of the *Washington Post*.

Despite his success, Bush worried more as his business grew, eventually developing bleeding ulcers. "I would worry a lot," he said. "I'd keep a lot inside me."

By 1953 Bush and John Overbey decided to merge their business with another independent oil company that had offices right next door. The partners were Bill and Hugh Liedtke, two lawyers who saw there was more money to be made in oil than in the courthouse. Each side put $500,000 into the new business. They called it Zapata Petroleum, after *Viva, Zapata,* a movie then playing in the Midland theater about Emiliano Zapata, the Mexican rebel leader who fought for land reform in the early 1900s.

The Liedtkes were not the type of men who drank liquor straight from the bottle. Like Bush, they came from a privileged background. Their father was chief counsel for Gulf Oil, and they had attended private high schools and Amherst College.

Johnny Hackney, who runs Johnny's Barbecue in Midland, remembers Bush, the Liedtkes, and others like them who hung out at his restaurant in the early 1950s.

"We had a bunch of Ivy Leaguers come to town then," he said. "They were all hard-working, aggressive, ambitious. Those Yankee boys were something else. I remember George Bush when he worked on the big oil rigs, worked in the warehouses, when he used to come in here dirty and sweaty."

With $1 million in funding, Zapata was profitable from the start. At the same time, the Bushes were movers and shakers among Midland's 25,000 residents. Allday said that George "helped start the YMCA, establish three banks, worked in the cancer crusade, United Way, Community Chest." He became a director of one of the banks.

George also coached Little League, and both the Bushes taught Sunday school at a Presbyterian church. By 1953 they had a second son, John Ellis Bush, called Jeb.

During those years George was gone much of the time, as were the other oilmen. Hugh Liedtke, who eventually became head of Pennzoil, recalls the Midland times as "hard on the girls" because they were left alone so much of the time with houses full of children.

"We would sit up on an oil well all night, stay out in the field several days," Liedtke said. "Then we would come home, covered with grease."

Barbara has said many times since that while she enjoyed those years in Midland—typical of the life many young wives led in that era—she also had resentments.

"I had moments where I was jealous of attractive young women out in a man's world," she said. "I would think, well, George is off on a trip doing all these exciting things and I'm sitting home with these absolutely brilliant children, who say one thing a week of interest."

But she is not one to complain about her life for long, and her strong belief that children need a mother nearby while they are young helped tremendously. "There's a time for babies, a time for growing," she said. "I just happened to lie dormant in rather important years and I might regret that. But I don't think so."

She was, by all accounts, a superorganized mother. She kept up the house by herself before George was earning enough money to hire household help. She went to the Little League games and kept score for her sons as she had for her husband earlier. And she was the family disciplinarian.

"She may be a lot of people's grandmother, but she was our drill sergeant when were growing up," said son Jeb.

It was Barbara who dealt with the day-to-day problems. She recalls a time when young George was spanked with a board by the school principal. George senior was out of town at the time, but when he learned about the incident he was furious. He sent his wife to school to complain.

Barbara said she told the principal, "My husband's going to kill you. He's out of town, but he's coming home to kill you immediately."

The principal defended his action, saying young George had disrupted his music class by painting a mustache on his face. He was sent to the principal's office as punishment, but instead of being contrite, he "swaggered in as though he had been the most wonderful thing in the world." Fearing the boy would become the class clown, the principal swatted him on the bottom with a board.

"And before I left that school, I thought the principal was right," Barbara said. "First of all, he hadn't bruised him or he hadn't hurt him. He'd hurt his feelings. . . . you don't want the class clown, you want a kid who's going to do his best . . . and I backed the principal. And then I had to explain to George."

Such minor problems cropped up all the time, and like other parents, the Bushes learned to cope. But nothing in their experience prepared them for the heartache to come.

In the spring of 1953 young George was six years old, Pauline Robinson—called Robin—was three and one-half, and John Ellis—Jeb—was still an infant. Barbara, busy with the new baby, didn't notice the small bruises on her daughter's legs, but she became concerned when Robin began moping around the house, no longer interested in active play.

"I may go out and sit in the grass and watch the cars go by or maybe I'll just lie in bed," Robin told her mother one day.

Barbara took her little girl to the family's pediatrician, Dr. Dorothy Wyvell.

Dr. Wyvell examined Robin, took a blood test—and asked Barbara to come back that afternoon with her husband. Of course that set off alarm bells, and Barbara quickly telephoned George. When they returned to the doctor's office, she met them with moist eyes.

"I'll never forget it," George said. "We walked in and the first thing, she pulled a Kleenex out of the box and just kind of wiped her eye. Then she said, 'I've got some bad news for you.' "[5]

Dr. Wyvell told the Bushes that Robin had an acute case of leukemia.

Neither George nor Barbara had a clear idea what leukemia was. They asked what the treatment would be. Dr. Wyvell told them there was nothing they could do—Robin's case was very advanced and she would not live much longer. The doctor advised the Bushes to take their little girl home, make her comfortable—and let her die.

"She said, 'Number one, don't tell anyone. Number two, don't treat her. You should take her home, make life as easy as possible for her, and in three weeks' time, she'll be gone,' " Barbara said.

Reeling with shock, the Bushes went home and blurted out the tragic news, so that shortly everyone in the neighborhood knew. The next day they flew to New York to consult with George's uncle, Dr. John Walker, a cancer specialist. He urged them to try to save Robin's life.

Robin was admitted to Memorial Sloan-Kettering, a top

New York research hospital, and was given a new cancer drug that helped.

For the next seven months, Robin was in and out of the hospital, flying with her mother back and forth between New York City and Midland, Texas. When Barbara and Robin were gone, neighbors helped George take care of the two boys, but eventually Dorothy Bush sent a nurse to fill in the gaps.

The drug Robin was taking worked well enough that she sometimes appeared to be a normal child—a hazel-eyed blond charmer.

"One day when she was in remission I took her down to the bank," George said. "We walked down there from the office . . . and they said, 'Where's the little girl who was so sick?' And here she was, she looked so beautiful, just like she was at the peak of her life."

But Robin's leukemia never went into complete remission.

"I remember her very clearly because she was one of those adorable children you can't forget," said Dr. Charlotte Tan, one of the doctors who treated Robin. "She always was a mature child. It takes a really big girl to tolerate an oxygen tent and all that when you're three years old."

During this period, George Bush began going to church by himself early in the morning to pray.

"I can tell you that there was no one for us to turn to but God," he said. "And I really learned to pray. I would slip into our church sometimes when no one was there. I would ask God why? Why this little innocent girl?"[6]

Barbara said that when the church custodian discovered Bush was stopping in every morning around 6:00 A.M. before work, he told the church minister. From then on, Barbara said, "The minister then came every day. He didn't say anything. He just was there."

The Bushes' hopes were raised briefly when friends telephoned to say they had heard a radio report that a doctor in Kansas City had found a cure for leukemia.

"Poor George got on the phone and called and called until he got the doctor," Barbara said. "George had gotten his hopes up so."

During the long days and nights at the hospital, the Bushes talked and prayed together and, in their typical fashion, tried to find the silver lining in a heartbreaking situation. They took comfort in their many blessings.

"We looked around and nobody had what we had," Barbara said. "They either didn't believe in God, or they didn't love each other or they didn't have other children or they didn't have brothers and sisters. In a way it was good for us because we realized we had much more than anybody else."

Robin died on October 11, 1953, about seven months after her leukemia was diagnosed. Her parents, both with her at death, can still see the bruises that covered an entire leg and the "100 or so" ulcers she had on her stomach at the last.

They donated her body to research. "First of all, I know there's a God and secondly, I know Robin left," Barbara said. "We both had that feeling that she wasn't there. We combed her hair and she wasn't there."[7]

Barbara said that she was the strong one in the family while Robin was alive. George would cry—she wouldn't let him get teary around Robin—but she never did. After Robin died, however, Barbara crumpled.

"I hadn't cried at all when Robin was alive," she said. "But after she died, I felt I could cry forever."

Once she was back home in Texas, she wanted to retreat from the world. "I nearly fell apart," she said. "I couldn't put my right foot in front of my left."

In a speech at the Republican National Convention in 1988, Barbara recalled how her husband gave her strength during those dark days. "He held me in his arms and he made me share it and accept that his sorrow was as great as my own," she said. "He simply wouldn't allow my grief to divide us . . . push us apart, which is what happens so often where there is a loss like that. And for as long as I live, I will respect and appreciate my husband for the strength of his understanding."

Young George also helped his mother. After Robin's death, she lavished attention on her two sons, almost fearful to let them out of her sight. Then one day she overheard George tell a friend, "I can't play today because I have to be with my mother—she's so unhappy."

At that point, Barbara said, she realized she had to pull herself together for the sake of her family. And gradually, she did.

Fifteen months after Robin's death, the Bushes had another child, Neil. Twenty-two months later, in October, 1956, they had a fourth, Marvin.

By this time, the family fortunes had improved and Barbara had help taking care of her active brood. She had a full-time housekeeper, Julia Mae Jackson, and a part-time baby-sitter, twenty-four-year-old Otha Taylor.

Mrs. Taylor recalls that when she arrived at the Bush home for an interview, Julia Jackson warned her she probably would not get the job because Mrs. Bush already had interviewed many prospects and rejected all of them.

"She called me in, we sat down and talked," Otha Taylor said. "She wanted to know if I had any children. I said no, but my sister did and I spent most of my time baby-sitting."

During the interview, Mrs. Taylor said, she felt comfortable—"I liked her right away"—and she was hired. She said she and Mrs. Bush got along well. "She will really let you know about it if you've done something wrong, but it only lasts for a few minutes. She was good about that."

The year was 1957, almost four years after Robin's death, but Otha Taylor said, "They were all still grieving." Every time the subject came up, she said, Mrs. Bush would say, " 'What I'm going to do, I'm going to keep trying until I get another girl.' "

Otha Taylor worked five hours a day for the Bushes. She came at two o'clock each afternoon, took the younger children to the park, brought them back to the house for a light supper, and then gave them baths and got them ready for bed. At that point, Mrs. Bush took over, reading the little ones good-night stories before they fell asleep.

Between six o'clock and seven, Mrs. Taylor said, she didn't have anything to do, since her job was strictly child-care. So, although she was paid to work until seven o'clock, Mrs. Bush told her she could leave after she finished giving the children their baths.

"Mr. Bush came in one day and wanted to know where's Otha? She told him. He said, 'What? She can sit up and read a book or something. She's being paid until seven o'clock and she should stay until seven o'clock.' "

Mrs. Taylor said her initial reaction at this dictum was anger.

"This made me mad at Mr. Bush, so I told my brother. I said, 'Mr. Bush is a real tight, stingy man.' I told him what happened."

To her surprise, Mrs. Taylor said, her brother agreed with George Bush. "He explained to me that Mr. Bush was paying me and the money wasn't what he was concerned about, it was just doing the job."

Mrs. Taylor, who in later years became a quality control technician at Mobil Chemical in Temple, Texas, said she came to appreciate that point when she got into the work world. "Going through working life, I understood what was happening here," she said. "I learned a great lesson from Mr. Bush."

Mrs. Taylor said she spent most of her time at the Bushes' with Jeb, who was four, and Neil, then two, while Mrs. Bush concentrated on her infant son Marvin.

"Now Jebbie, I kind of enjoyed him," Mrs. Taylor said. "He was very observant. They were very, very easy to take care of. Their parents spent a lot of time with them. They were very mannerly kids even at that age."

She said the young Bushes had no idea about race differences, and Jeb tried to puzzle out the variations in skin color one day while sitting at the table with Otha.

"Julia was a brown-skinned person and I am black and Julia's husband, Willie, was black," Mrs. Taylor said. "I can remember one day Jebbie and Neil were sitting at the table having their snack. Jebbie said, 'Otha, me and Neil is the same color and you and Willie are the same color.' I said, 'What color is Julia?' " And that stumped him. "They didn't know the differences in races and color."

But questions of race loomed large in the rest of the country, brought into sharp focus by the school desegregation efforts and riots in Little Rock, Arkansas, that summer of 1957. Mrs. Bush, Otha Taylor, and Julia Jackson had firsthand experience with the racism still prevalent across the land when they drove from Texas to Maine with the three youngest Bush children.

"Mr. Bush didn't go for it at all," Mrs. Taylor said. "He didn't want her to drive that far. He wanted us all to fly."

But Otha Taylor and Julia Jackson were afraid to get on a plane, so George Bush bought a new station wagon for the six travelers—Mrs. Bush, her two helpers, Jeb, Neil, and baby Marvin. Young George, busily involved in baseball tournaments, was to fly to Kennebunkport later with his father.

Mrs. Taylor recalled how excited she was when the trip began. It was to be an adventure for all of them. Their first stop was to be Oklahoma City, and Mr. Bush made reservations at a hotel ahead.

"When we arrived at the hotel, we went through the back to get unloaded," Otha Taylor said. "Mrs. Bush went in while we were sitting out with the kids. When she came back out, she said, 'Girls, we're having a little problem.' She didn't say what it was. She said, 'I'm going to call Mr. Bush.' "

The problem was that the hotel didn't allow blacks. But after George Bush spoke with the hotel manager, he agreed that the family could stay—as long as they kept out of sight.

"We went in and Mrs. Bush said, 'Girls, they're not going to let us eat in the restaurant. So all of us are going to eat up here. We're going to enjoy ourselves.' "

As Otha Taylor remembers, Barbara ordered a huge spread in an effort to make the occasion more cheerful— ham, turkey, and lots of treats.

"We had to leave early in the morning," Mrs. Taylor said. "The man could have lost a lot of business by letting us stay there. I don't know what Mr. Bush did [to convince him]. I guess he did the same thing he did over there in the Persian Gulf."

The next stop was Kansas, where Barbara planned to visit friends. They were able to find a motel to stay in, and Barbara thought she had solved their problems by buying uniforms for both Otha and Julia. "She said someone had told her if you traveled in uniform, they wouldn't give us any trouble."

But that didn't prove to be the case. When dinnertime came, Julia and Otha took Jeb and Neil to the motel restaurant while Mrs. Bush was getting ready to visit her friends.

"We went in and sat down," Mrs. Taylor said. "And nobody paid us any attention for about ten minutes. Then a woman came over and said they didn't wait on colored."

With young Jeb full of questions, the party went back to the motel room. "Mrs. Bush was very upset and she called the manager," Mrs. Taylor said. "He told her they didn't serve black people and she said, 'How's my girls and kids supposed to eat?' He said we could get room service. She told us to order big, to get anything we wanted."

Barbara still recalls that trip with anger.

"I was just sick," she said. "We had those babies with us. You know Little Rock had happened in the middle of the trip so it polarized people. It was disgusting."

On the trip home, she recalled, "Howard Johnson's had that year . . . opened up to everybody. So they saved our lives."

Mrs. Taylor said the situation was not much better even

when the party arrived in Greenwich, Connecticut, to visit Dorothy and Prescott Bush. The Bushes suggested that Otha and Julia might enjoy seeing the sights of Greenwich and recommended a ferry ride. So they bought their tickets and got in line. But when they reached the ticket taker, he told them they couldn't ride—no blacks allowed.

This time, however, Julia Jackson decided she wasn't going to be denied, and the magic of the Bush name came to her aid. She asked the man if he knew Senator Prescott Bush. "She said we are here with his daughter-in-law and they sent us down here to ride the ferry." The reaction was swift: "He let us ride that ferry all the evening. We didn't even have to pay."

Despite these ugly incidents, Mrs. Taylor said the trip was interesting. In Connecticut, she and Julia stayed at the home of the senior Bushes, observing the family and listening to the political talk. Prescott Bush made a strong impression. Mrs. Taylor said, "That's where I decided I wanted to be a Republican."

The group traveled on to the Bush home in Kennebunkport for summer festivities. There was the usual boating and sports and games, but Otha Taylor recalled that the young children balked at spending time with their great-grandmother, an elderly woman who maintained a formal house not designed for active preschoolers.

However, young George, being the oldest, was required to go along to dinner at his great-grandmother's while the younger children got to stay behind and enjoy a deep-dish blueberry pie.

"His father said he had to come because he was a big boy. He and his father were always tussing about something," Mrs. Taylor said. "George didn't like to go there because Granny Bush had a very formal table. And she only served chicken salad sandwiches."

Mrs. Taylor worked for the Bushes for only six months. Shortly after the trip to Maine she decided to get married. She said Mrs. Bush was not pleased at her departure, but she understood. And for years, "she kept in touch with me. She would send me pictures at Christmastime . . . in fact, I still get them."

During these years, George Bush's oil business continued to prosper. In 1958 he moved the company headquarters to Houston. A year later the Bushes had one more child—a much-wanted girl—Dorothy Walker Bush. The family was complete now. And Barbara was immersed in her life as wife and mother.

Short Stubby Arms and Sticky Kisses

When George Bush is asked what he is most proud of, he says it is the fact that his five children still come home.

None of the Bush children is estranged from each other or from their parents. Everyone in the family appears to like everyone else, and though the relationships are not perfect or problem free, the whole family pulls together in time of triumph and crisis—and often, just for fun.

The fabric of these relationships is Barbara Bush's finest accomplishment. While the children were growing up, George was often away working, either at his job or in community or political affairs. "Dad was the chief executive officer, but Mother was the chief operating officer," said Jeb.

It was left to Barbara to set the tone for the family, impose the day-to-day order and discipline, and provide the hugs, encouragement, and sympathetic ear.

"I think what made for a great family experience was that there was always a feeling of warmth," Marvin Bush said. "When I came into the house, I felt that. I knew I was surrounded by people who loved me. At first I really wasn't that aware of it; I thought everyone else had the same situation. But when I started bringing friends home, I realized that we had something special."[1]

Barbara recalled with some pride that the neighborhood children often drifted to her house and played in the Bush backyard—a pool helped draw a crowd. She devoted all her energies to her husband, her children, and her household. Never one to say she has regrets, she nevertheless remembers those years with mixed feelings.

"It was a period for me of long days and short years," she said in a 1985 speech, "of diapers, runny noses, earaches, more Little League games than you could believe possible, tonsils, and those unscheduled races to the hospital emergency room; Sunday school and church, of hours of urging homework, short chubby arms around your neck and sticky kisses and experiencing bumpy moments—not many, but a few, of feeling that I'd never, ever be able to have fun again, and coping with the feeling that George Bush, in his excitement of starting a small company and traveling around the world, was having a lot of fun."

When she was left alone with a houseful of small, active children, she said, "There were days I thought I would scream if the children didn't say something intelligent."

When George was home, he played with the children, caught up with their lives, and added a lively presence to the family mix.

But while he was away, Barbara was left to deal with the problems.

"When Jebbie was twelve he walked peculiarly; the doctor thought it might be a rare bone disease," she said. "George was away, so my friends held my hand. But it turned out to be only an infection in his heel. Neil had an eye emergency and I had to rush him from Midland, Texas, to Houston, but it turned out to be nothing."[2]

When the children needed discipline, Barbara said, she was "the enforcer," even spanking them occasionally. "I didn't spank hard, but I spanked," she said. "I would scream and carry on."

George didn't get into these frays because he often wasn't on hand at the moments the misdeeds occurred. But the children still feared his anger, which he expressed psychologically rather than physically.

"Mom was always there," Neil said. "My father was the ultimate authority whenever there was a conflict which couldn't be resolved at the mom level."

"I don't remember him punishing us," Jeb said. "But just knowing he was disappointed in me was enough. I couldn't stand it."

Added Barbara, "The way George scolded was by silence or by saying 'I'm disappointed in you.' And they would almost faint."

George W., the oldest son, was especially vulnerable to his father's disapproval. He still remembers a time when, as a young man, he walked out on a summer job on an offshore oil rig a week early to be with his girlfriend, thus failing to fulfill his commitment.

"Well, my father found out about it," he said. "Follow-through and commitment were among the things he strongly believed in. So I was called into his office in Houston. He looked at me and said, 'Son, you agreed to work a certain amount of time and you didn't. I just want you to know that you have disappointed me.' "

Young George said that was about the harshest his father got—no yelling but a lot of moral suasion. So he left the office feeling guilty and rotten. But, typically, George Bush did not stay angry for long. About two hours after the office confrontation, he telephoned his son and invited him—and the girlfriend—to a Houston Astros game.

The two men had a more serious confrontation when George W. was twenty-six. By then the family had moved to Washington and George W. was on his own. When he came for a visit one afternoon, he took his fifteen-year-old brother Marvin to a friend's house, where they both had too much to drink. On the trip home, George W. ran into a neighbor's garbage can while turning into the Bush driveway.

It wasn't long before the father asked his son to step into the den. George W. recalls being drunk and having a belligerent attitude as he entered the study. "I hear you're looking for me," he said to his father. "You want to go *mano a mano* right here?"

The boys are quick to admit they had rough edges when they were young, despite the *Father Knows Best* image the Bush family projects.

"I think we were all rebellious when we were in the rebellious stage," Jeb said.

"We weren't all goody two-shoes," Neil said, referring to his high school years in the early 1970s. "I don't think we were hippies but we weren't unaffected by the times we were raised in. I remember being in Washington for high school when the city was on fire and those were troubling times, the Vietnam War, the protests. No one [in the family] was actively protesting, but when you're in a school environment, you can't help be affected by what goes on around you."[3]

He said he and his brothers also engaged in a lot of competition, friendly but intense. "We played basketball and we'd throw elbows at each other and duke it out. After it was over we'd always be friends." But, he added, "No one in our family likes to lose."

Doro, the youngest child and the only girl, wasn't so much involved in the fray, and she had an easier time with her father than her brothers did. For her, he was the proverbial soft touch.

"I hate to say this but Dad let me do anything I wanted," she said. "Mom was the one who had all the rules. Dad always gave in. My friends were always jealous. They'd say, 'God, you've got the greatest dad.' "

The children don't remember their parents fighting over discipline methods or money or any of the other things that typically cause family squabbles. Barbara Bush said they did argue in their early years together, but George also used quiet disapproval in these matchups, which put his wife at a disadvantage.

"What's the point?" she said with some of the exasperation she must have felt years ago. "He would just let you flail and flaunt . . . I mean, it's no fun to argue in a one-sided argument. He knows what he thinks and he's perfectly willing to let you scream and yell, but I just gave that up. That was a waste of our energy."

She also sometimes despaired of getting George to take the children's misdeeds seriously, as she illustrated in a speech at the 1988 GOP convention:

"I called George one day when the boys were small and said, 'Your son just hit a ball through the neighbor's upstairs window.' And he said, 'My gosh, what a great hit.' And then he said, 'Did you get the ball back?' "

George W. said he realized when he was growing up that his mother "put her relationship with her husband above her relationship with us." But, he said, that didn't cause resentments because she was so generous with her time for all family members.

"I played a lot of Little League, and I still have vivid memories of seeing her sitting at our games, keeping score," he said. "She bent over backwards for me and my brothers, especially in our love of sports."

When the boys got older, she was nice to their girlfriends too, although she recalled that some of them were "real dogs." But remembering the warm reception she got from Dorothy Bush even before her engagement, Barbara said, "I treated them all like they were neat, nice people."

Barbara has an easy relationship with her oldest son, who has a feisty outspoken nature and quick wit similar to her own. "We fight all the time," she said. "We're so alike in that way. He does things to needle me, always."

George W. is the only Bush child born on the East Coast, but he is the most confirmed Texan of the bunch. He lived in Midland from the time he was two until eighth grade, a small-town boyhood full of baseball, bicycling, swimming, and neighborhood buddies. He was almost grown by the time his father started out in politics.

George was the child most affected by Robin's death. He was seven years old when she got sick; and number-two son Jeb was just an infant. George still vividly recalls the day he realized his three-year-old sister had died.

"I was at school that day in the second grade and I can still see in my mind's eye my parents pulling up in the parking lot. I was carrying a Victorola back to the principal's office with a kid named Bill Sallee. My parents had been in New York City at the Sloan-Kettering clinic with Robin and they had just returned. I remember looking in the car and thinking I saw Robin in the back. I thought I saw her, but she wasn't there."[4]

By the time the family moved to Houston, George W. was ready for high school, and he followed the family pattern, going first to Andover, then to Yale. But his experiences were much different from his father's.

Where George Bush had grown up with chauffeurs who deposited him each day at Greenwich Country Day School, George W. went, on his own power, to San Jacinto Junior High in Midland, Texas. Thus Andover, whose upper-class students were mostly from east of the Mississippi, came as a culture shock; it was where George W. first discovered his distaste for the effete East.

At Yale, George Bush was Phi Beta Kappa but George W. got mediocre grades. "I was never a great intellectual," he said. The campus in the late 1940s was full of World War II veterans, some of them, like Bush, war heroes. But George W. was at Yale during the Vietnam War, when campuses across the country were alienated from government and bogged down in protests. Many young college men sought to avoid the draft; few were willing to volunteer for the front in such an unpopular war.

George W. didn't join the protests of the era; he signed up for military service, learning to fly fighter planes just as his father had done. But the son chose the Texas Air National

Guard instead of the navy, and although he was in a program that rotated National Guard planes to Vietnam, he was not called.

In his late twenties—after the *"mano a mano"* incident with his father—George W. decided to get a master's degree in business and he was accepted at Harvard. He got the degree, but didn't have an easy time. It was the height of Watergate and his father was part of the Republican establishment.

Nancy Ellis, the president's sister, living in nearby Boston, recalls the period as a tough one for her nephew.

"You know Harvard Square and how they felt about Nixon," she said. "But here was Georgie, his father head of the Republican National Committee. So he came out a lot with us just to get out of there."

Like his father, George W. had no desire to work on Wall Street, and he was even more eager to leave the East Coast. Repeating the journey his parents had made three decades earlier, he drove to Texas, deciding he too would try his entrepreneurial skills in Midland. He started out researching mineral and land records and eventually went into business for himself.

Young George did not have the same success in oil that his father had—he later complained "I'm all name and no money"—and he is teased by friends and relatives for his skinflint ways. But he has always been solvent and able to attract investors—he put together a group that bought the Texas Rangers baseball team in 1988—and he is interested in politics. He ran unsuccessfully for Congress in 1978 and considered entering the race for Texas governor in 1990. With George Bush in the White House, however, Barbara publicly urged her son not to run, fearing "a filthy campaign. I thought the hurt would be enormous."

He didn't run.

George W. didn't marry until he was thirty years old; Barbara called it a red letter day when he finally announced his intention to marry the daughter of a Texas contractor,

Laura Welch, a librarian he had met just three months earlier. Said Laura of the brief courtship, "We were both thirty and had had a lot of single years. We were glad to find each other."

Jeb, the second-born son, is seven years younger than George. He considers himself "the serious one" of the Bush siblings, maybe because he spent scarcely any time as the family baby. His brother Neil was born when Jeb was just two years old, and Marvin came along a year after that. Neil says that "although George might dispute this, Jeb and Marvin are probably the brightest of the boys."

Jeb, Neil, and Marvin, so close in age, sometimes hung out together. Jeb recalls a weekly neighborhood newspaper they put together—and sold for a nickel a copy.

The family lived in Houston during most of Jeb's childhood, years in which George Bush was prospering in the oil business.

Jeb followed his father and older brother to Andover for prep school, but his experience there was not a happy one. It was the late 1960s and the political disaffection that had afflicted college campuses was also alive at Andover. "The school was rebelling against itself," Jeb says. "Our class particularly. I think the school hit bottom with us."

By his senior year, though, Jeb had found an interest that would last a lifetime—Mexico. Taking part in a work-study course titled "Man and Society," he worked in a Mexican village and helped build a schoolhouse. One evening he was invited to the home of a Mexican girl who was dating another Andover student. Jeb sat down next to the girl's sister, Columba Garnica, and reacted to her much the way George Bush had responded to Barbara three decades earlier. "Boom, I was gone," Jeb said. "She was the first girl I ever loved and the last." He returned to Andover realizing his carpentry skills would never amount to much, but his respect for Mexico would be abiding.

Columba gave Jeb a goal in life, something that the eastern establishment at Andover had failed to instill. During his last trimester, he made straight A's for the first time. And, like his father, he went through college—not Yale but the more culturally comfortable University of Texas—in two and one-half years.

"I wanted to get it over, get on, get married," Jeb said. "She gave me a sense of purpose."

Jeb told his parents about Columba but was slow to let them know how serious the relationship was. It wasn't until Christmas vacation of 1974—Jeb was twenty-one by this time and out of college—that he introduced her to the Bushes and informed them he planned to be married in Austin two months later. Whatever fears Jeb might have had about his parents' reactions dissolved. They didn't object to the marriage, and Columba immediately found herself brought into the family circle, especially welcomed by Barbara Bush.

Jeb and Columba sometimes speak Spanish at home, and although Jeb was raised as an Episcopalian, their three children—George P., Noelle, and Jeb—are baptized as Catholics. The oldest of Jeb's children, George P., has an especially close relationship with his grandfather, who calls him P. George Bush was hurt and amazed during the 1988 presidential campaign at the outcry that developed when he affectionately referred to these three grandchildren as "the little brown ones."

Jeb and Columba live in Miami, where he works in real estate and is politically active, having served as Florida's secretary of commerce in the late 1980s. Columba, who does not have a paying job, said that contrary to public expectations her family isn't rich and doesn't live extravagantly.

"People think we should have a swimming pool full of gold," she said. "They don't understand we're just as normal as can be. I cook and clean, Jeb wakes up every morning and goes to work. We just kind of hide out down here."

Like many middle children, number-three son Neil has had the most trouble of the five Bush siblings. As a child, he had severe reading problems, which he managed to cover up until second grade.

Barbara recalled sitting down with him one day when he was sick and trying to read with him. He didn't seem to know the words. She telephoned his teacher, who wasn't aware of any problem, so Barbara visited the classroom.

She found that when Neil was called on to read, his classmates fed him the words. On his own, he couldn't do it.

Tests revealed that Neil had dyslexia, a disorder that makes it difficult for children to put letters together to form words and to sound out words from a group of letters.

With great energy, Barbara went after solutions. She hired tutors, found books with large print, put together practice tapes, and offered endless encouragement.

"Dyslexia, back in those days, was not well known," said George W. "Mother worked hard with Neil, disciplining, training, encouraging. She was the one who really spent the time making sure that Neil could learn to read the basics."

Still, Neil had trouble in school and continued to dislike reading unless the subject was sports. He went along with his mother's program, but he said, "For years and years I hated it. I hated reading. The only thing more painful in my life than reading was once when I broke my front tooth."

He remains grateful to his mother, however, for bolstering his self-confidence, praising him for the things he did well instead of concentrating on his deficit reading. "She loves gardening and I loved helping her because she made me feel I did it better than anyone else," he said. "She brought that out in me. To this day, I don't feel handicapped. I have all the confidence in the world because of her."

The Bushes were in Washington by the time Neil was ready for high school. He was enrolled at St. Albans, a good private school with many children from socially prominent families, but one that didn't have the same cachet as Andover, where George Bush and his first two sons had gone.

Neil's teachers told Barbara he might not be able to handle college, but she refused to believe this negative message and so did Neil, who has a dogged and optimistic personality. He graduated from Tulane University in New Orleans in 1977 with a bachelor's degree in international relations and went on to earn a master's degree in business two years later.

Neil met his wife Sharon, a schoolteacher, while he was campaigning for his father in New Hampshire in 1979. A local Republican introduced them with the idea of generating a romance, and it worked—they married less than a year later.

Sharon and Neil settled in Denver during the early 1980s. Neil, like his father, planned to make his fortune in oil. He and two friends started an oil and gas exploration firm with a $300,000 stake from two larger energy companies. But they drilled thirty-one holes without ever striking oil or gas.

Despite his lack of success in the oil business, Neil became a well-liked figure in Denver and was sought after by people attracted to the Bush name. In 1985 he joined the board of the local Silverado Banking, Savings and Loan Association at the invitation of its politically ambitious president, Michael Wise.

Silverado failed and was taken over by federal regulators in December 1988. Neil, as an outside director of the board that controlled Silverado, was in trouble. The federal Office of Thrift Supervision, which regulates savings and loans, found in April 1991 that he had violated conflict-of-interest rules while serving as a Silverado director. The agency ruled that if Neil wanted to serve on a savings and loan board in the future, he would have to get advice from a lawyer about conflict-of-interest rules. It also said that he would have to disclose all his financial and business interests to federal regulators for a year. Five Silverado officers were prohibited from working in the industry in the future.

Neil was accused of failing to tell the Silverado board of his relationship with two Colorado developers, Bill Walters and Kenneth Good. The men had invested in Neil's unsuccessful oil company, JNB, and later received approval for loans or lines of credit from Silverado. Neil abstained from voting on the loans.

The director of the Office of Thrift Supervision, which

issued the sanctions against Neil, was Timothy Ryan, who had been a legal advisor to George Bush's presidential campaign. Even though the sanctions had been endorsed by a trusted friend, the Bush family felt that Neil had been singled out for prosecution because he was the president's son. George W. said that his brother was "getting hosed because his father is president of the United States, period . . . there's not a devious bone in his body."

The president said, "It's tough on people in public life, to some degree. I've got three other sons and they all want to take to the barricades, every one of them, when they see some cartoon totally demeaning of the honor of their brother. I say, 'You calm down now. We're in a different role. . . . You can't react like you would if your brother was picked on in a street fight.' "

But despite these brave words, the family was heartsick.

"If he weren't my son or George's son I don't think you would ever have heard his name," Barbara said. "I'm sorry for him because it's very costly for him. I think he feels this is hurting his father, which is ridiculous. One might think his father is hurting him . . . one of the prices children have to pay."

A week after the federal ruling against Neil, Barbara flew to Denver to speak to a local charity that he was supporting.

Neil himself was angry and also hurt by the way federal prosecutors had pursued him. "I probably am guilty of not being the savviest political guy in the Bush family," he said. "I didn't do anything wrong. I acted properly as a director. I was as fit as any director to sit on the board."

During the controversy over Silverado, Neil was also investigated by a congressional committee for another business deal, but the panel found no wrongdoing.

The second investigation was launched because Neil and a colleague had invested $3,000 in a Denver oil company—Apex—in May 1989 and a federally subsidized small business fund had put up $2,300,000. Neil, as president of the company, was paid $160,000 a year although the company never made a profit. He resigned from Apex in April 1991, the same month that the savings and loan ruling was issued against him.

Marvin, the youngest of the Bush sons, has stayed away from both oil and politics. He is credited by his siblings with the best sense of humor and is considered by many people to be the most personable of the Bush children. Like his father, he has hundreds of friends and an easygoing charm. His business is finance and investment, which is just fine with his parents.

"Never once growing up did I feel pressure from either of my parents to be something I'm not," he said. "That to me is one of their greatest accomplishments. All their children are extremely different, and they appreciate us for who we are."

Just twenty-one months younger than Neil, Marvin keenly felt the presence of three older brothers during his childhood, and the competitive atmosphere sometimes got to him.

"I remember one afternoon up in Maine," he said. "My brother George and I were playing tennis when things got a little tight on the tennis court. I was about ten years younger than he was and it got to an especially tense point in the match. I think I was fairly brash and was making sure he knew exactly what the score was. The next thing I knew he was chasing me up a fence."

Perhaps because of his struggles to compete with so many older siblings, Marvin eventually improved his tennis game to the point where he is the acknowledged family champ—he's the one George Bush calls when he wants a challenging game.

"I guess you could say I was the classic little brother, always trying to emulate my brothers, always trying to hang around," Marvin said. "Sometimes, in a particularly feisty mood, I'd accuse my parents of adopting me, just to get their attention. It never worked."

He also recalled being upset as a child at the time his mother devoted to charity—time he thought could have been better spent on him.

"I remember being jealous when my mom would run off to the Washington Home," Marvin said. "I thought she spent an inordinate amount of her time there. It wasn't until I was older that I appreciated what she told me, that to live a complete life, you need to help other people."

Marvin has stayed especially close to his parents. He went to college at the University of Virginia in Charlottesville, just two hours from Washington, D.C. When he fell in love with a fellow student, Margaret Molster, he talked with Mom and Dad before deciding to marry her.

"I was fairly young, twenty-four, and I wanted to feel comfortable and get some reassurance with what I was planning to do," he said. "They said I'd better marry Margaret because the chances were slim I'd find someone as special again. That turned out to be excellent advice."[5]

Because she had ovarian cancer, Margaret, who is trained as a teacher, cannot bear children, but she and Marvin adopted two infants, Marshall in 1986 and Charles in 1990. They live in Alexandria, Virginia, a Washington suburb.

Marvin said the strength Margaret drew from overcoming her childhood illness helped him cope when he developed life-threatening ulcerative colitis in 1986 and had to have his colon removed. In May that year Marvin had an ostomy, an operation that creates an opening in the abdomen for the passage of waste. The waste goes into a pouch attached to the body at the opening.

George Bush was vice president when Marvin had the operation, and both he and Barbara spent a lot of time at the hospital praying for their son, an ordeal that reminded them of the loss of Robin more than two decades earlier.

"I can't help but think that while my mother was with me during that period she might have had some flashbacks to twenty-five years ago when she was with my sister," Marvin said.[6]

Even several years after Marvin's illness, Barbara Bush still gets teary-eyed when she talks about it. "Since then we've put things in perspective," she said. "We've realized there are worse things than losing an election. Marvin's very valuable to us. We knew it, but we didn't know how valuable. I just think that our fresh perspective had something to do with Marvin."

Marvin himself felt depressed after the operation. He was only twenty-nine years old and feared the bag at his waist would mean an end to sports and perhaps affect his relationship with Margaret. But, cheerful by nature, Marvin turned his thinking around before long. "I thought of the alternative, the unbearable pain, the increased risk of colon cancer associated with longstanding colitis, and possibly death. Wearing a pouch seemed a small price to pay for the privilege of leading a normal, productive life."[7]

He said he was especially encouraged by a call from a man who had had the same operation several years earlier, Rolf Benirschke, a former place kicker for the San Diego Chargers who had gone on to a television career. Rolf assured Marvin he could still take part in sports, have a good relationship with his wife, and lead the same active life he led before. And he got Marvin interested in helping other people who have had the operation.

"Since then, I've been pretty actively involved in going to the United Ostomy Association convention down in New Orleans," Marvin said. "They have a support group there that helps people on the verge of having this operation deal with the problem in a number of different ways."

Although all the Bush children say they try not to trade on the family name, Marvin, like his mother, found that his high profile could be used to spotlight good works. "After a colostomy some people hide in their houses for years without coming out—thinking that they're so unappealing or unattractive to others," he said. "I can show them that it doesn't matter at all."[8]

He says his mother is thrilled when he goes on the stump

for a good cause: "She's more excited when she hears I gave a speech in North Carolina to the ileitis-colitis foundation than if I get a bonus at work."

Marvin is three years older than his sister Dorothy, called Doro by the family, and admits he spent much of his childhood concocting ways to torture her. He is embarrassed by that today, but Doro seems to have survived intact. She has an especially strong relationship with her father, being the only surviving girl in the family, and she unabashedly adores him.

"My dad would just spoil me with love," she said. "There's something about our relationship I can't explain. He was just a soft touch with me."

The poignant memories of Robin may have been one reason. Doro says that when her father tucked her into bed at night during childhood, he would tell her about Robin "and we would both cry."

She recalled with amusement the time when she was ten or eleven and her father played a joke on her. "He called me from the office and said, 'Hello, little girl. This is the telephone repairman. I'm testing your phone. Hold the phone away from your ear because there might be a loud noise.' I held the phone out for a real long time until finally Mom asked what on earth I was doing. She caught on right away."

Doro has fond memories of her childhood—the felt Christmas stockings decorated with sequins that Barbara Bush made for each child, the thrill of getting soaked in George's speedboat off the coast of Maine, the fun she had living with her parents at the Waldorf-Astoria in New York City—like Eloise at the Plaza—and being driven by a chauffeur to the UN School, while George Bush was ambassador to the UN.

But Doro was always shy and self-conscious. When the chauffeur drove her to school in New York, she asked to be dropped off a block away so no one would see her in the fancy car. When the Bushes first moved to Washington, she feared she wouldn't be dressed right, so her father took her across the street to ask a girl her age what the current fashion was. It turned out to be the right move; the short socks Doro wore in Texas looked nothing like the knee socks girls in Washington favored.

Like Barbara, Doro went to high school at an exclusive girl's school, Miss Porter's in Farmington, Connecticut. She recalled how excited she was one day when her father, in New York for a speech, invited her out to dinner.

"I thought I was really hot stuff going there to meet him," she recalled. "We were going to spend the night at the Waldorf and after the speech, he took me to the 21 Club for dinner. I thought that was the neatest thing in the world. We were sitting there at dinner and all of a sudden Dad started to fall asleep because he was so tired. I was so excited and my dad was sleeping. It was funny."[9]

Doro had no great interest in a career, but she did earn a degree in sociology from Boston College. While she was vacationing in Maine after her sophomore year in college, Doro met William LeBlond, and she said, it was "love at first sight." They married as soon as she got out of college and had two children, Sam and Ellie.

Doro fondly recalls the birth of her first child and a special trip her father made to see her when he was busy running for reelection as vice president.

"It was 1984, right in the middle of the campaign, and I was in the hospital having Sam," she said. "It was a big baby, ten pounds, and I was feeling pretty rough. The nurse looks out the window and says, 'Oh, there are police dogs and police and all these men in suits running around.' I said, 'Oh, my, it's my dad.' Then there was a knock on the door and there he was. I couldn't believe he came in the middle of the campaign. We walked down together to see Sam and it was the greatest day of my life."

Afterward her father sent her this letter:

Dear Doro: Monday was a very special day in my life. Sam is beautiful. He has two great parents who will give him love all his life. Seeing that little guy made many thoughts run through my head. Thank God he's strong and well. Thank God he's born to a family of love and kindness and caring. Then I must confess, I thought—I am sixty—it doesn't feel old but it is pretty old; and here's Sam, one day old, just starting out in life, with much joy and happiness ahead of him and a mother who has given her own Dad nothing but happiness and love; and a father who will be at his side teaching him about decency and honor and the importance of family. Sleep on fat little Sam—a lot of fun awaits you and when you hurt, your beautiful, wonderful mom will hug you. Devotedly, Dad.

Early in their marriage, the LeBlonds lived in Maine—Doro figured her parents would eventually retire there and she wanted to be near them. Bill LeBlond ran a construction firm and Doro did bookkeeping for him but mostly concentrated on raising her children.

The marriage was short-lived, however; Doro was divorced after her father became president, and she took her children and moved to Washington to be near her parents once again.

"My daughter spent lots of time with me when her marriage broke up," Barbara said. "Now she's gone back to that neighborhood where she grew up [in Washington] and gotten a little house and put her children in school there. She's doing great."

Betsy Heminway, who is Sam's godmother, says that Doro and her mother are close, although they don't have the same relationship as Doro and her father.

"She and her father are very, very close; not that she and her mother aren't . . . Doro is very sensitive and sometimes that's tough. Also, with four older brothers, there's the good news and the bad news. . . . I would probably say George and Marvin are the closest to her. Of course Marvin is now living in Washington. The two youngest [Doro and Marvin] weren't that close, but now they've become close."

Doro overcame some of her shyness through a desire to help her father in his political campaigns. During his unsuccessful 1980 bid for the Republican presidential nomination, she took a course in typing and shorthand so she would have some skills to offer the campaign and she worked in his New England office.

But, like her mother, she was initially shaky on the campaign trail. When Bush's aides persuaded her to speak at a tea for elderly women, she blanked out and sat down shaking. By the 1980 campaign, however, she had become more confident. She helped organize caucuses in Maine early on, then began traveling. By the time the Republican National Convention was held in New Orleans, she was happily speaking out on her father's behalf every chance she got.

Barbara is defensive about her children—admittedly so. She reacts like a mother bear whenever they are criticized.

"My children have had only minor problems," she says. "They haven't had any real problems. And don't forget. I'm right there with them every step of the way. . . . They're all wonderful kids. We've always been very conceited about how wonderful our family is."[10]

Political Wife

George Bush won the first political race he ever entered. The year was 1962 and Republicans in Houston, hoping to end decades as the underdog party of Texas, saw the young eastern oilman as someone with a future. They asked him to run for chairman of the Harris County Republican Party.

Bush was eager to get into politics, and he accepted right away, figuring the work he put in at the local level would pay off if he sought a higher office later.

Barbara remembers the campaign as a dirty one. She was shocked to find hate mail shoved right under the door of her house, but to her surprise, she enjoyed other aspects of politics. After fifteen house-bound years centered on children—with George away on business much of the time—she found it a pleasure to be at her husband's side in a fast-moving campaign.

The Bushes methodically visited all 189 precincts in Harris County. Barbara sat on stage while George gave his speech—the same one over and over again. She did needlepoint to help pass the time.

But where she really became an asset was in the mix and mingle before and after the speeches. Her outgoing personality quickly won the candidate friends, and she was good at remembering names and faces and events connected with them, a much-valued skill in a world where who you know and what they think of you counts more than anything else, except for money.

Still, Barbara remembers her failures somewhat ruefully. Witty and opinionated, she was not accustomed yet to biting her tongue. "The first time I campaigned I probably lost George hundreds of votes," she said. "I'm not only outspoken, I'm honest."

Bush had been asked by moderate Republicans to enter the race to keep the right-wing John Birch Society from taking over the GOP in Harris County. The Birchers fought back, even dragging Barbara's father into the race.

They noted that Marvin Pierce was president of the McCall Corporation, which published *Redbook*. And *Redbook,* the John Birch Society said, was a Communist magazine. Some voters in the far reaches of rural Texas who had never seen the popular woman's magazine might even have believed it.

By 1964, two years after he won the Republican Party chairman's post in Harris County, Bush got GOP backing to run for the U.S. Senate. His opponent was a liberal Democrat, incumbent senator Ralph Yarborough.

Barbara worked door to door in the Senate campaign, sometimes wearing a nametag that gave only her first name because she wanted to know what people really thought of George Bush. Too often, the answer was that he was just another upstart Republican, reason enough in Texas at the time to vote against him. Lyndon Johnson was elected president that year and Yarborough won reelection handily, defeating Bush 1.46 million votes to 1.13 million, or 56 percent to 43 percent.

George Bush took defeat well, according to Barbara, but she didn't.

"He was wonderful," she said. "He got right on the phone the next morning and thanked everybody who helped him, you know, cheering them up. I was terrible. I went out and played tennis and tears were flowing down my face."

Doro Bush, just five years old at the time, recalls breaking down in tears also when she learned her father had lost. "I said, 'Dad, I'll be the only one in school who has a father without a job,' " she said.

Not to worry. George Bush still had part ownership of a profitable offshore oil business and enough money to keep his large family comfortable for many years.

It was during that campaign that Barbara gave up on attempts to dye her hair, which had turned white when she was only twenty-eight during Robin's illness.

"I began coloring it myself, but it turned every color but the warm brown I wanted," she said. "So back when George was running for the Senate, I went to the beauty parlor and said how bad my hair looked. The beautician said, 'Let's try this rinse called Fabulous Fawn.' So we rinsed with Fabulous Fawn and off I flew to East Texas to campaign. . . . It was a hundred and five degrees in that plane. I asked the pilot to turn up the air-conditioning, but he told me it had just gone out. And my Fabulous Fawn began to run. It ran down my neck, my ears, my cheeks, and my forehead. I began to blot myself with Kleenex, used all that up, then started on toilet paper. I spent the whole flight mopping myself up."[1]

Despite his defeat in the Senate race, Bush was not ready to give up on politics. He ran for the House of Representatives from Harris County in 1966 and won—the first Republican ever elected in the district.

The victory meant another move for the Bush family. They had lived in Houston for seven years; now Washington would be their home.

By this time, only three of the five children were still living with their parents full time. George W. was at Yale and Jeb was getting ready for prep school at Andover.

Barbara enrolled her three youngest in elite Washington schools. Doro, seven years old, went to the Cathedral

A young Barbara with her dog Sandy. Mrs. Pierce sent this photo to George Bush when he asked for a photo of Barbara during their courtship. *Courtesy Rosanne M. Clarke.*

Friends come in all sizes. From left, Posy Morgan Clarke, Barbara, Lucille School-field, and Kate Siedle. *Courtesy Rosanne M. Clarke.*

From left, Barbara, Posy Morgan Clarke, and Kate Siedle as statues in a pond. Posy Clarke describes this photo as "the only time Barbara had to look up to me." *Courtesy Rosanne M. Clarke.*

Barbara, far left, as Beatrice in her high school production of *Much Ado About Nothing.*

Barbara and George Bush on their wedding day, January 6, 1945. *Courtesy the White House.*

Barbara and George at Yale. She kept score for the baseball team. *Courtesy the White House.*

The Bush family in 1964: George and Barbara seated with Doro and Marvin. Standing left to right: Neil, Jeb, and George W. *Courtesy the White House.*

Election night, 1966, after George's election to the United States Congress. *Courtesy the White House.*

In China under a photograph of Mao Tse-tung. Barbara described the year in China as one of the happiest of her life. *Courtesy the White House.*

A Bush family portrait, 1979. Top, left to right: Marvin, 22; George, 3; Jeb, 26; George; George W.; George's wife, Laura. Bottom, left to right: Jeb's wife, Columba; Noelle, 2; Dorothy, 20; Barbara; Neil, 24. *Courtesy the White House.*

ASHLEY HALL *Newsletter*

Academic Excellence for Four Generations

WINTER 1980   172 Rutledge Avenue, Charleston, South Carolina 29403

A CONVERSATION WITH BARBARA BUSH

Some weeks before the Presidential election on November 5, we contacted Mrs. George Bush (**Barbara Pierce '43**) by letter requesting a telephone interview for our Winter Newsletter. We knew our readers would be interested in her reactions to the past year's activities and to the results of the election. We were granted permission to do the interview and then learned that Ambassador and Mrs. Bush would be in Charleston on November 1 for a Republican Fundraising Breakfast. We were able to arrange a personal meeting with Mrs. Bush and spent a delightful half-hour talking with her. On Thursday after Tuesday's election, Mrs. Bush called us from Los Angeles where she and her husband were visiting with President-elect and Mrs. Reagan. The interview which follows is a transcription of that telephone call. WCSC Radio graciously taped the interview for Ashley Hall and in return had the opportunity to further question Mrs. Bush.   — *The Editors*

DEE DEE: "So you say your life has changed, Mrs. Bush."

MRS. BUSH: "Well, only because we won and quickly got on an airplane and flew out to be with the Reagans for lunch yesterday and some talk, and today George has a press conference. Then we are going to fly back to Houston, Texas, tonight — and I think after the week-end we are going to try to go off for a little rest."

DEE DEE: "I am sure you can well use it. I know it has been very exciting for you. Now, I know you have traveled all about the country, and having seen the United States and the grass roots of this country, so to speak, what do you perceive to be the real mood of the majority of the country? Are you encouraged or discouraged?"

MRS. BUSH: "We never thought the country was sick at all, we always thought there was a great lack of leadership, and of course the mood of the country really is one of wanting to get inflation under control, and I think the people were a little bit frightened because they did not see us going in a direction that was going to solve the problem of the economy. The country is good, the people are fantastic! And I really think the big surprise of the election was, No. 1, the mandate that Governor Reagan got; No. 2 was the terrific turnover in the Senate, the first time, I think since 1956 that the control of the Senate has changed parties. That will make a tremendous difference because it means that the staff will change, and that is very important."

DEE DEE: "That's wonderful. I think that will be supportive for your policies and whatever it is that you, as a group, decide to do. Do you feel, then, that your contact with the people, and the mood, and certainly the mandate of the country in the victory has influenced or changed in any way your perception of what must be done by the Reagan-Bush White House?"

MRS. BUSH: "No, because you know Governor Reagan ran a big State, and I think he knows that jobs are very, very important, and I don't think it has changed our perception really — the problems that were there today, and more so — inner-city problems, lack of jobs, lack of incentive in business, in . . . . oh just lack of incentive has been very obvious to us from the beginning. I hope we can change all that."

DEE DEE: "Was there anything you found surprising as you traveled about the country, that was unexpected and surprising to the good or to the bad?"

MRS. BUSH: "No, I wasn't surprised because George and I have moved twenty-seven times since we have been married, but I am always sort of overwhelmed by the goodness of people — always — generosity, lovingness — I was not surprised at all by that."

DEE DEE: "To what do you attribute your obvious self-confidence, and certain ability, and willingness to travel the campaign trail across the country?"

Barbara Pierce Bush - 1943
(Courtesy of the Charleston News & Courier)

A newsletter from Barbara's high school alma mater featured the First Lady on its cover in 1980.

Barbara Bush wearing her signature three-strand pearl necklace. *Courtesy the White House.*

School; both twelve-year-old Neil and ten-year-old Marvin were at St. Albans, a prominent boy's school.

George had bought a house sight unseen from a retiring senator, but once the rest of the family members settled in, they discovered it had neither enough space nor enough light. It fell to Barbara to find something better.

Barbara had joined a study group organized by Shirley Pettis, the wife of another new Republican congressman, Jerry Pettis. The two women soon became friends, and one afternoon Barbara told Shirley she had found a house she liked.

"They were in a house and we were in a house and neither of us was happy," Shirley Pettis said. "She said she found one that interested her and she wondered if I could just hop in the car and look at it and so I did. I thought it was an absolutely superb house."

What Barbara had found was a pair of new homes at the end of a cul-de-sac in northwest Washington near the National Cathedral. The house she liked was a three-story brick with a small front yard and a patio in back. The second new home, a mirror image, was just across a courtyard, separated from the first house by a brick wall.

Shirley urged Barbara to buy the house, and Barbara in turn urged Shirley to buy the one next door.

The next day Barbara got George to look at the house she liked, and they signed a contract for it on the spot. Shirley and Jerry Pettis bought the house next door, but they took a little longer to make a decision.

"I took my husband over and I took the children and they couldn't imagine why I couldn't make up my mind as fast as Mrs. Bush," Shirley Pettis said. "They let me know about it. But we did buy it a couple of months later."

Barbara set out immediately to fix up the house and the garden and to get to know her neighbors, among them Supreme Court Justice Potter Stewart and Franklin Roosevelt, Jr.

"Bar was a very outgoing, neighborly type," Shirley Pettis said. "She soon knew everybody on our cul-de-sac. She walked the dog, C. Fred, so she would meet everybody."

Justice Stewart's wife, Mary Ann, had met George and Barbara earlier while Prescott Bush was in the Senate. Mrs. Stewart recalled George's mother Dorothy telling her "You'll just love my daughter-in-law. I know you'll hit it off."

Dorothy Bush was right. Mary Ann, widely known as Andy, found herself attracted to Barbara immediately. The two shared an unusually high energy level, an emphasis on family, enjoyment of politics, and husbands with interesting and very public jobs. They became close friends and remain so today.

Before the Bushes moved into the neighborhood, however, longtime residents had been looking unhappily at the two new houses at the end of their lane.

"It was an area in our neighborhood where there had been an empty plot and somebody had built two houses facing each other," Mrs. Stewart said. "We were not at all pleased with the fact that the empty lot was gone."

Neither did the neighbors like the style of the new homes, which looked like town houses. "They seemed to be more modern," Mrs. Stewart said. "The rest of the houses were considerably older. They had been there and settled for a long time."

So it came as a pleasant surprise when the Bushes moved in, soon followed by the Pettises.

The new families added sparkle to the neighborhood. Barbara, in typical fashion, had her house amazingly organized in no time. "Within a week after she moved in she looked more settled than I had in four years," Mrs. Stewart said.

With a housekeeper to help inside, Barbara devoted a lot of time to the garden, mulching, mowing, weeding, and even doing tasks that would daunt many a lesser gardener.

"As soon as the weather was propitious, the garden was planted," Shirley Pettis said. "She had hers in beautiful,

blooming order far before I did. She's extremely action oriented, and she's so organized that I've always said she could
easily run General Motors or the Pentagon."

Barbara excelled at putting the garden together in an attractive way, able to imagine what it would look like when
completed.

"She has a real sense of what looks good in a garden,"
Shirley Pettis said. "Her mental eye could just envision how
each flowering bush was going to look. And furthermore,
she would do a lot of the work herself. She had a wonderfully cooperative back. She'd bring in great loads of all the
textured things that have to go into the soil."

"She's a prodigious do-it-herselfer," Mrs. Stewart said.
"She thinks nothing of putting in a dogwood tree or moving
bushes. She loves hands-on."

The Bushes, still lonesome for Texas friends, began to
entertain frequently once they got the house and garden in
order, most often with the kind of informal barbecues they
had been giving ever since Midland.

Barbara made salads, soup, and casseroles. George cooked
hamburgers on the grill—but Barbara got them all ready
beforehand. "She always had things masterfully organized,"
Shirley Pettis said. "It was always on paper plates and cups
and napkins. There'd be a big trash can immediately outside
where we could dump everything.

"The dessert was always something very special, often-
times meringues. Paola [the Bushes' longtime housekeeper]
made wonderful individual meringues and she would fill
them with ice cream or berries."

The barbecues became a regular Sunday afternoon event,
fondly recalled by guests even years later.

"It was always great fun," Mrs. Stewart said. "They invited all kinds of people—people who worked for them or
with them early in Texas, people they met around the world,
relatives—thousands of relatives it seemed, they're a big family—their children and everybody else's children who were

the same ages. It was just very nice, a buffet, and then we'd sit around and talk, politics and interesting things around Washington.

"The thing that always interested me was not only their friends and all the people that came and went, but it was always very orderly. It was civilized."

Shirley Pettis said it was the talk that made the parties special, "all sorts of ideas exchanged, the bouncing of ideas one to another. It was really a fascinating sort of get together."

At the same time, said Janet Steiger, whose husband, William, was first elected to Congress the same year as George Bush, "There was never anything forced. It was very easy. There was always a football game going in the background."

George was an immediate success on Capitol Hill. The thirty-nine other freshmen Republicans in the ninetieth Congress elected him to be their leader, and thanks to his father's friendship with Democrat Wilbur Mills, George was appointed to a coveted spot on the Ways and Means Committee. He was the first freshman of either party to serve on the powerful tax panel in sixty years.

Barbara was a success also, quickly plunging into activities with wives like herself whose husbands had just been elected to Congress.

"Barbara was a very sought after member of the group of nineties club wives," Janet Steiger said. "She was then as she is now an extremely warm and outgoing person, and she made friends instantly."

Mrs. Steiger recalled with amusement how Barbara had taken a liking to one of her ideas and improved on it.

"I started the idea of a slide show of little-known places in Washington," she said. "It prompted some interest among some of the ninetieth wives and I showed it to them, being quite proud of it of course. Bar immediately took what I thought was quite an accomplishment and made mine look silly. Typically, she got into what I thought was most effective, the gardens of Washington. Then she got into the churches, making mine look at best like a raw beginning.''

She laughed. ''It's not surprising that nobody remembers I ever did it. Whatever anybody else does, Bar makes better.''

The Washington slides, she said, made an effective campaign tool for the wives, who often were asked to speak in their home districts. ''People are interested in Washington and most of them bring their youngsters. It was a nonpolitical piece, which meant the audience could be anything.''

But Barbara initially was fearful of showing her slides to an audience. ''When she came to Washington she was positive that she could not do that,'' said Shirley Pettis. ''Then one of the clubs in Texas asked her to show her pictures on Washington. I remember telling her that anybody who could preside over a dinner or a luncheon table with so much wit . . . you'll be a big hit.''

Barbara did make the speeches, but she still worried a lot. Shirley Pettis said she would get up early and ''five o'clock in the morning I'd see her light in her den.'' She was working on her speeches.

One reason Barbara was popular with the other congressional wives was that she made time for them when they were in need, as Janet Steiger fondly remembers.

The Steigers were from Wisconsin and while they were in Washington, Janet became pregnant. When she went to a local hospital to have the baby, the only relative she had in town was her husband, so she was surprised when a nurse told her a close relative had come for a visit and even more surprised when Barbara came trotting in.

''Barbara was always a rock,'' Mrs. Steiger said, ''somebody you'd want with you in a tight spot. She of course sent my husband away. She conferred with the medical types. It was obvious to her nothing was going to happen at that minute. She sent him back to his office [on Capitol Hill] and she then summoned him at the appropriate time.''

Barbara could also be a demanding friend, not for her own

needs but as a recruiter for her charity work. In the early 1970s when she was spending a lot of time at the Washington Home, a health-care center for the chronically ill, Janet got a phone call from her. "We're going to need a little help doing the Fourth of July picnic" for residents of the home, Barbara said. "You're home, so here are the directions."

Janet Steiger didn't argue. "This was a home for the incurably ill. I think it takes a very special person to dedicate themselves to that," she said. "Bar really adopted a couple of folks who were multiple sclerosis victims and she was just simply devoted. She's never been on a board that I can think of where she was just an honorary. Bar was a working member."

With that in mind, Janet Steiger responded readily to the holiday call. "It was the Fourth of July, they were shorthanded. We went over to dish out the hot dogs and baked beans. You don't think about whether you're a volunteer . . . get with the program."

When Bill Steiger died of a heart attack in 1978, both George and Barbara flew to Wisconsin to be with Janet, who had to decide whether to run for her husband's congressional seat and what would be best for her young child. She said Barbara helped her put the questions into focus, and she ultimately decided she didn't want to be in Congress while her son was young.

"It put a focus when it's very difficult for you to focus," Janet Steiger said. "She's an extraordinarily sympathetic friend. Her tack is to see what she can do something about."

Old Texas friends also found Barbara a help when they came to town. Jessica Catto, whose husband Henry was appointed ambassador to the Organization of American States, came to Washington with four small children and was worried about finding good schools for them.

"Barbara was the one who drove me around to get oriented," she said. "She was a congressman's wife at that point. She's that way for her friends. She just was there."

George Bush was reelected to Congress in 1968 without

any opposition and probably could have gone on serving in the House for many years. But Texas Republican leaders and President Nixon believed that Senator Yarborough was more vulnerable than ever by 1970, and they urged Bush to take him on again.

In his autobiography, *Looking Forward,* Bush said that among the people he consulted before making a decision was Lyndon Johnson. Although Johnson was a Democrat who would never have endorsed Bush, a Republican, as a politician Johnson didn't like Ralph Yarborough.

Bush said he flew to Johnson's ranch for a talk about politics and he got the advice he was seeking. He remembered the conversation this way: "Son, I've served in the House. And I've been privileged to serve in the Senate, too. And they're both good places to serve. So I wouldn't begin to advise you what to do, except to say this—that the difference between being a member of the Senate and a member of the House is the difference between chicken shit and chicken salad. Do I make myself clear?"[2]

Bush decided to make the Senate race, even though it meant giving up a safe seat in the House. To his surprise and chagrin, however, Yarborough was defeated in the Democratic primary that year by a conservative, Lloyd Bentsen. Years later Bentsen would lose in a race to Bush—in 1988 he was the vice presidential candidate on a ticket with Michael Dukakis—but in 1970 Bentsen won the Senate race by a comfortable margin, 53.4 percent to 46.6 percent.

Barbara, at the end of an exhaustive campaign, took defeat hard. "When I called her up after the loss of the Senate election she couldn't stop crying," sister-in-law Nancy Ellis said years later.

But the disappointment was short-lived. President Nixon, having urged Bush to take a chance in the Senate race, was ready with a consolation prize. Would Bush like to be U.S. ambassador to the United Nations?

Yes indeed.

The Bushes had spent four enjoyable years in Washington

in a quiet, tree-filled, suburbanlike neighborhood. But they were accustomed to moving, and New York City was an attractive offer. Their new home was the elegant Waldorf Towers in the Waldorf-Astoria Hotel, which the government kept as an official residence for the ambassador. All the boys were away at school by this time, and Doro was the only child still at home, so a spacious hotel suite provided plenty of room for the family, despite the lack of a kitchen.

With her customary zeal and organization, Barbara set to work immediately making the government-issue apartment a home.

"Bar has a way of bringing fresh potted plants and flowers in, mostly flowers," said Shirley Pettis, who with her husband was a house guest of the Bushes in New York. "She's very feminine in that respect. She loves flowers and soft colors around her. She likes art that reflects the soft colors and flowers and children playing. She's really quite feminine in many of her artistic pursuits. Whatever home she's in she's going to have blooming flowers. It's such a signature with her."

"She converted a rather drab hotel apartment into quite a sparkling residence," said W. Tapley Bennett, one of Bush's top aides at the United Nations. "One room was all in greens and whites; that was entirely her decoration."

As visitors entered the residence through a foyer, they were greeted with examples of American artistry—displays of Steuben glass and American paintings borrowed from New York's top museums. American wines were served in the formal dining room.

"She added a touch of personal interior decorating, she put a little color and life into it," said Ed Derwinski, who was the congressional delegate to the United Nations at the time. Derwinski also recalled a Christmas party Barbara held especially for children of the United Nations staff.

Barbara attended the UN sessions, bringing her needlepoint along, but stayed away from the government office where George worked. "She would come and sit in the delegates' gallery on the side," Bennett said. "She was very supportive of her husband."

With a busy social life, her husband always nearby, and so many interesting people around, Barbara came to love the New York assignment.

"I would pay to have this job," she said. "It was like being taken around the world to meet people from a hundred twenty-eight countries and yet never having to pack a bag or sleep in a strange bed."

She also made time for the volunteer work she has done wherever she lives. In New York she spent Tuesday and Thursday mornings helping out at Sloan-Kettering Cancer Institute, where Robin had been treated.

And she dutifully accompanied George to the many diplomatic functions he was required to attend. She recalls one evening especially that turned out to be quite embarrassing—and it was all her husband's fault.

"To this day, he doesn't realize how sore I was at him," she said. "It was really horrible. We had a night where you charge from reception to reception. I'd worn a short, bright-red cocktail suit with gold threads. It could not have been redder, or louder. After three receptions, I said, 'Where to now?' George said, 'Come on, I'll tell you about it later,' and we raced up some stairs. Next thing I knew, we were in a funeral parlor. The ambassador of a Central American country had died. All the ladies were properly dressed in black and I was there in bright red. We were thrust into the center of the lights as the television announcer said, 'And here comes the United States ambassador and Mrs. Bush.' I couldn't wait to get out of there."[3]

Bush liked the New York assignment as much as Barbara did and delved into it with his usual enthusiasm. By tradition, whenever a new ambassador arrived at the United Nations, he makes a call on the U.S. ambassador. Bennett said Bush used these occasions to learn more about the world,

getting out history books and atlases to steep himself in information about the newcomer's country, in preparation for
the meetings.

Bush had the United Nations job from March 1971 to
January 1973, far too short a time to suit Barbara. But, as
always, she was ready to move on when her husband's career
was at stake.

The change came shortly after Richard Nixon began his
second term in the White House. He wanted someone he
could trust to head the Republican National Committee in
Washington, an important political post, and he offered Bush
the job.

Although investigations already were being made into the
Watergate break-in at the time, there was no indication that
January of the revelations that would follow just months
later. Bush agreed to take the job because it was what the
president wanted him to do. He didn't really have much
choice.

The next two years were a dismal time for the Bushes and
other Republicans in Washington. The Watergate scandal
swept through the capital and dominated political and social
life in the city.

By the spring of 1973, just three months into the job, Bush
was put in the position of defending Nixon and the White
House against increasingly serious charges. He stayed loyal
right up to the end, joining the chorus calling for Nixon's
resignation only on August 7, 1974, after it became clear that
the president would be impeached if he did not leave volun-
tarily.

Upon Nixon's resignation, Gerald Ford became president.
Bush felt that his hard-time duty as Republican National
Committee chairman and his popularity within the GOP had
earned him the right to be named vice presidential candidate,
but Ford chose Nelson Rockefeller instead.

As a consolation prize, Ford offered an ambassadorship,
mentioning that the prestigious posts in both London and

Paris were opening up. But neither post interested Bush. Both England and France were firm allies, and the job of ambassador in either capital would be largely a social function. Instead, Bush asked for something more challenging—China.

Although Washington and Beijing did not have formal diplomatic relations at the time, the two countries did maintain "interest sections" in one another's capitals. Richard Nixon had "opened" China several years earlier, and the effort to establish a good relationship with the Communist giant was still in the early stages. So China would be an interesting post. Ford agreed to give Bush the job. He would be the first top-level diplomat stationed at the U.S. mission in Beijing.

George and Barbara left Washington eagerly. Almost two years of Watergate had soured them on life in the nation's capital for the moment; they both felt the need to get away for a while, and China proved to be just the tonic they needed. The children, all in their teens or beyond, stayed in the United States at schools and with relatives and friends.

It was Barbara's first trip abroad and her first extended time alone with her husband in many years. She loved it.

It "was a whole new leaf in both our lives," she said. "Watergate was a terrible experience, so to go off to China and learn a whole new culture was beautiful. I loved the people. I loved the whole feeling."

They arrived in Beijing in October 1974. Their new home was an apartment in the Spanish-style compound reserved for foreigners. They had a household staff of six and enough room to entertain. But relations with the United States being what they were, there was little contact with Chinese, either government officials or the workers.

Early on, the Bushes decided to use their time to explore as much as they could. They gave up driving for the most part because few Chinese had cars. Instead they traveled by bicycle. They played tennis, read, and entertained visitors from the United States, including both Gerald Ford and Henry Kissinger, who considered China his personal preserve.

Barbara started a flowered needlepoint rug in China that would take her eight years to complete. She wove her initials into it in Chinese.

She also studied the country's history and art and took pictures of everything she could, later organizing them into a slide show. China, she said in later years, was the place where she began to look at herself more closely, the time when she "deep-delved."

"I don't mean to say that I didn't do a lot of things before," she said. "But I was always a nice little follower."

At Christmas that year George and Barbara were separated for the first time since they had married. Barbara returned to the United States to be with the children. George remained in Beijing, but his mother and an aunt arrived to keep him company.

During the summer of 1975, all the children except Jeb joined their parents in Beijing. Marvin, eighteen years old at the time, recalled later how bleak he found the Chinese city.

"My parents met us at the airport. All I remember about landing is how dusty it was," he said. "There was no grass . . . there was a lot of dirt in Beijing. It was a dirty city and I ended up getting a cough as soon as I got there. In fact, all of us did."[4]

But they were all there for a special purpose. Doro, who had not been baptized as an infant, celebrated her sixteenth birthday on August 18; she was to be baptized in Beijing—an unusual occurrence in Communist China.

The ceremony was held in the church used by the diplomatic community. Three Chinese Christian clergymen took part, an Episcopalian, a Baptist, and a Presbyterian. No other Chinese attended the ceremony, but representatives from the diplomatic community did.

Marvin, who stood in for absent godparents at the ceremony, described the church as plain and the organ as antiquated. But, he said, "it was moving to see people who had to make an effort to seek the place out . . . it was so humble and yet so powerful to see this happening in the middle of the largest Marxist nation in the world."

During his stay in China, Bush met with both Mao Ze-dong and Mao's successor, Deng Xiaoping. He and Barbara both developed an abiding affection for the country and its people, even though the appointment to Beijing lasted little more than a year. By December 1975 President Ford had asked Bush to return to Washington to become head of the Central Intelligence Agency.

Neither George nor Barbara was happy about this development. For one thing, it meant Ford did not want Bush on the 1976 presidential ticket. Vice President Nelson Rock-efeller had announced he would not be on the ticket in 1976, so that left an opening. But Ford wanted a running mate who would satisfy the right wing of the party since Ronald Reagan was prepared to make a challenge at the 1976 political convention. Ford gave the nod to Senator Robert Dole of Kansas.

Politics wasn't the only reason the CIA was unattractive. The agency had been involved in a number of questionable activities during the 1960s and the Vietnam War, leading Congress to launch several investigations that were still active in 1975. Whoever became director of the agency could expect to spend a lot of time on Capitol Hill answering questions and many hours at CIA headquarters across the Potomac River in Virginia trying to repair the agency's low morale.

Bush was aware of all these drawbacks, but he took the job anyway. He had always agreed to do what presidents Nixon and Ford asked—and besides, he had nowhere else to go at the time, politically.

The move back to Washington was a hard one for Barbara. For the first time, all her children were off on their own, leaving a void that hadn't existed in the excitement of China. When she got back to the United States, the women's movement was in full swing and even women who had stayed home much of their lives were getting jobs. In Washington, it took courage to tell someone at a cocktail party that you were a housewife; chances are, they would move away quickly, figuring you couldn't possibly have anything interesting to say.

"I think part of it was that the children were all gone and part of it was women's lib, which made that woman who stayed home feel that she had somehow or another been a failure," Barbara said.

Worse still, Barbara had become accustomed to talking regularly with George about the China job and spending a lot of time with him. When he became head of the CIA, there was little he could tell her about his work. And he worked long hours.

Barbara mentioned to Mary Ann Stewart that she felt left out of George's professional life for the first time. Mrs. Stewart, as the wife of a Supreme Court justice, had long since learned there were subjects she could not discuss with her husband and had come to accept that fact.

"I said you just have to go with it," Mrs. Stewart recalled. "If you marry someone who's going to do interesting things, you just have to."

What Barbara did not tell Mary Ann Stewart or Shirley Pettis or any of her other friends was just how depressed she was with her situation.

"About six months, maybe. I mean, we're talking major depressed," Barbara said years later. "And I didn't do anything about it except shake it off . . . I think maybe I was at 'that age' whatever 'that age' is. But it makes you much more sympathetic for people who have depression. It is not something you can just say, 'Now pull yourself together and get up and go.'

"I would feel like crying a lot and I really, painfully hurt," she said. "And I would think bad thoughts, I will tell you. It was not nice."[5]

In retrospect, Barbara thought she probably should have

talked with a doctor, but she didn't think about doing so at the time. "I gutted it out and poor George gutted it out. I told my doctor later, 'I came to see you once for a physical. You asked me how I was and I sort of cried. That was very painful for me,' and he said, 'Well, you didn't say anything. I just thought you were tired.' I said, 'Well, I was tired, but tired of hurting.' "

Shirley Pettis said that although Barbara is an outgoing person, she is also by nature private and never one to discuss her problems.

"I think politics definitely furthers that tendency to keep anything that might be negative, your family, your marriage, your general health, anything that's negative you don't talk about. I think it's hard because you keep everything within yourself. You just feel you can't say anything."

Finding herself unable to talk about the depression, Barbara decided to try work as therapy. She put in long hours at the Washington Home—"Boy, I just kept myself so busy, though"—which helped bring her out of the slough.

Although Barbara Bush is not an introspective person, she did a lot of thinking about her life during this time, about her role as a wife and mother and whether she had missed out by not having a career.

She concluded that the decision to stay home and raise five children had been the right one for her and her family. It had been the norm for women of her generation who married men capable of supporting them. She felt that the fact that the norm changed in the 1970s did not mean she had made the wrong choice.

The CIA years were not all negative for Barbara. Once she got over her depression, she again began to enjoy her friends.

In 1975, while the Bushes were in China, Jerry Pettis had been killed in a plane crash and Shirley had taken his seat in Congress. She recalled that by the time she started going out again, Bush was head of the CIA and the block on which they lived was the most secure in Washington—which complicated her dating.

"I remember my very first time I had a date after my husband's death," Shirley said. "The Bushes had just come back from China and I hadn't seen Bar yet."

Still feeling shy and uncomfortable with the idea of dating again, Shirley was chagrined when she drove up to her house with her date. "There was Bar sitting on the curb with Andy Stewart, like they were waiting with their tongues hanging out. I was just horrified."

Shirley got even. Years later, when she had remarried and moved back to her California district, she stayed active in Republican politics and sometimes had Barbara out to speak at political rallies.

"When I introduce her, I do it a little tongue-in-cheek with some saucy reminiscences," she said. "I'd maybe tell that story about her waiting for me on my first date, or irritating me to death by mowing the lawn when the gardener didn't come and she didn't like the way it looked. She did that a couple of times, which absolutely alarmed me."

Barbara filled her days in those years with her friends, her needlepoint, and her volunteer work. But by the late 1970s, this quiet life was coming to an end. George, who stepped down as CIA chief when Jimmy Carter became president in January 1977, had decided to run for president in 1980.

He started his campaign early, at a low level, traveling to Iowa and New Hampshire with just a couple of aides. But soon he had the entire family working on his behalf.

It was the beginning of something that would put Barbara's vaunted organizational skills and high energy level to a new test.

The 1980 Presidential Campaign

I n 1979 and 1980 Barbara Bush was on the road almost every day for two years, campaigning for her husband—first for president, then for vice president. Much of the time, especially in 1979, she traveled with just one aide.

Although she would have preferred campaigning with George, she knew that wasn't politically wise. While he had been in Congress for two terms and held high-level appointive jobs in Washington, he was little known outside Washington and Republican circles, so the Bush family needed to fan out to reach as many people as possible.

Since Republicans thought that President Carter was vulnerable, there was a lot of competition for the GOP presidential nomination—Ronald Reagan, senators Robert Dole and Howard Baker, and former Texas governor John Connally were among the candidates.

"It was pretty tough starting off with that field of candidates," said Andy Stewart. She recalled traveling with Barbara on one of her first campaign outings to nearby northern Virginia, which is just across the Potomac River from the Capitol but a maze of confusing streets to Washingtonians.

"We both got kind of lost getting there," Mrs. Stewart said. "It was one of the first forays starting out, a Republican gathering."

As the wife of a little-known candidate, Barbara could not attract a large crowd. Her audience generally consisted of a handful of Republican women meeting in someone's living room over tea and coffee.

During her travels, Barbara met up with people she knew wherever she could. In Connecticut, it was longtime friend Betsy Heminway, who remembers the early days of the campaign as a strictly informal affair.

"Barbara would say, 'Let's run into Talbot's. I need something to wear for next week.' It was that kind of thing. She never took herself too seriously. She would just be trying on things, saying 'I've got four lunches and an afternoon thing,' " trying to figure out what she needed.

"She wasn't particularly comfortable at the beginning," Betsy Heminway said. "Her vehicle at the time was a slide show of China. Where she'd go, she would give a slide show and that's kind of what I think got her going. That was her original vehicle to get into the swing of making speeches. It was received very well."

Aside from nervousness of public speaking, Barbara also had to contend with questions about her looks, foreshadowing the preoccupation with her white hair that developed during later campaigns. Mrs. Heminway recalled a fundraiser in Rye, New York, Barbara's hometown, where George's mother Dorothy was present. One of the guests, wanting to introduce someone to the older Mrs. Bush, took him by mistake to Barbara, saying "I'd like you to come over and meet George's mother."

"That had to be very tough," Mrs. Heminway said, "and boy, she handled it well."

Such remarks prompted some in the Bush campaign to suggest that Barbara dye her hair so that she would look younger. Although she generally went along with the campaign strategists, she firmly resisted when they tried to interfere in such a personal area.

"When George was first going to run for president, a member of our family said, 'What are we going to do about Barbara?' " she recalled. "I said, 'Funny, it doesn't bother George Bush.' "

As it turned out, her hair wasn't a problem, especially among the women's groups she spoke to most of the time in the early days of the campaign. Her outgoing personality and superior social instincts helped her establish a quick rapport with audiences, and her confidence grew.

"She's a good speaker," said Pete Teeley, who was Bush's press secretary during the 1980 campaign. "She's very composed in terms of what she wants to say. She has a real presence. She works hard and she was a first-class campaigner for George. She was a significant asset to him because, you have to remember, that nobody knew who the hell he was."

The Bush children also tried to help remedy the "George Who?" problem. Teeley said that Neil was involved "to a considerable" degree and Jeb, Doro, and Marvin to lesser degrees. George W., who would be a major player in later campaigns, "didn't do much" in 1980, Teeley said. "He was trying to make a living at that time."

Oddly enough, George Bush credited all his children with active parts in the campaign when he wrote his autobiography. But he made no mention of the long months that Barbara had put in.

Barbara saw both George and the children occasionally while she was campaigning, but most of the time she was on her own with one aide, Becky Brady (now Becky Beach). Becky was the granddaughter of Mary Louise Smith, a political activist who had succeeded Bush as head of the Republican National Committee.

Becky herself was just getting into politics as a volunteer in Bush's political action committee in Houston when Barbara approached her about the travel job in 1978.

"My grandmother is a friend of theirs but she did interview four people," Becky said. "We hit it off. One thing she said to me before she hired me was that she appreciated the fact that I had volunteered for her husband."

The two began traveling together in January 1979, four months before George Bush had officially announced his candidacy for the GOP presidential nomination. Their first trip was to Birmingham, Alabama, where Barbara showed her China slides to a garden club.

"It was the first group of people and she was nervous about doing it," Becky said. "She wasn't accustomed to speaking. But she was fabulous. She put the audience at ease. It was new to her and she didn't realize how well she was doing, but they loved it."

Longtime friend Janet Steiger said Barbara's China slides were particularly popular because they showed American audiences what life was like in a country that had been closed to Westerners for decades. "After all, they [George and Barbara] were effectively the first American representatives back in China in the lifetime of most Americans. It was for most people the opening of a mystery."

Barbara soon got into a routine on the campaign trail. She and Becky would fly to a city and hook up with a local Republican, who acted as guide. They would do five or six events a day, each one lasting about an hour, then repeat the whole process the next day.

"It was every day," Becky said. "We would basically come home, maybe for a weekend, but it was never very long."

They each carried their own luggage, helping one another where they could. Barbara had a blue hanging bag that she called Big Blue and another case with multiple zippers. She tried to coordinate her clothes colors so she wouldn't have to carry so much.

"She and I both tried to pick a color so we could mix and match everything," Becky said. "She had a steamer and she would steam her clothes in her hotel room."

Barbara always carried along panels of the family rug that

she had started to needlepoint in China. She worked on it in any spare moments she had, traveling in the car or plane and in her hotel room.

"That was one of my biggest responsibilities, not to leave or lose that rug," said Becky, who often wound up carrying the panels in a tote bag. "She worked very hard on it. She kept a very good log as to what animal or flower she had done on a certain day." Many of the designs were in celebration of family events—births, elections, graduations.

Becky did needlepoint as well. "I had done needlepoint when I was in school," she said. "In all our car trips, we'd always work on that. We got to be best friends really, traveling like that when it was just the two of us for so long."

They also collaborated on thank-you notes. Barbara sent thousands of them, and Becky helped her get names and addresses and put them in a directory.

"We'd try to get everybody's names and she would do thank-you notes practically before we were out of town," Becky said. "Each one was personal and she wrote them all herself. I didn't write them for her."

Barbara also took along a supply of paperback books wherever she went. When she finished one, she would leave it on an airplane for someone else to read, which also meant that she didn't have to carry it any longer.

Although the campaign days were long, Barbara always got up early enough to have some private time in her hotel room to read, work on needlepoint, and exercise. "She had a coil to make her own coffee in the morning," Becky said. "She'd get up about five-thirty. We'd frequently leave the hotels about seven-thirty."

Barbara did her own scheduling with help from state parties and old friends. "They've [the Bushes] got friends all over the country and a lot of their friends would help us," Becky said. "They would pick us up and drive us across the state."

She recalled a typical week they spent in Michigan arranged by Patsy Caulkins, who had lived next door to the

Bushes while George was a student at Yale. Mrs. Caulkins was not politically active, but still was able to put together a full schedule of activities.

Barbara and Becky stayed overnight at her house in Grosse Point, then got up at six the next morning for a two-hour drive to Ann Arbor, where they had breakfast with a group of Republicans, not all of whom knew who George Bush was. "President of what?" one was overheard asking. After breakfast, Barbara had an interview with the local newspaper, where the reporter did not know who George was, and she met with the mayor and toured city hall. Lunch was in Lansing.

The next day she traveled to Grand Rapids, where Mrs. Caulkins's sister-in-law had arranged a fair-size party. Barbara also had an interview at a local TV station. Later in the day, Mrs. Caulkins drove the party to Muskegon, where a friend of hers had agreed to throw a wine and cheese party for Barbara and also had invited all three women to stay overnight at her house.

Knowing what a busy day it would be, Mrs. Caulkins had packed a picnic lunch and en route to Muskegon she hunted for a roadside picnic table. Finding none, she simply pulled the car off the road and everyone ate. Before long, a policeman came by and stopped when he saw the car. He asked if everything was all right.

"I introduced Mrs. Bush and told him her husband was running for president," Mrs. Caulkins said. "He wasn't very impressed."

At the wine and cheese party, she noticed that both Barbara and Becky were writing down names. She was pleased to discover a few days later how many people had received a personal note from the candidate's wife—even the teenage girls who had served the hors d'oeuvres were remembered.

After Muskegon it was on to Midland, Michigan, where a woman the Bushes had known in Washington gave a coffee for Barbara. She had lunch with several of the women who attended and gave a short talk as well. That afternoon Mrs.

Caulkins drove Barbara and Becky to Bay City for a party and TV interview, then on to Flint for another gathering "all before supper."

On the final day of the visit, Barbara visited a shelter for abused women in Pontiac, and she attended two parties in nearby Birmingham, Michigan.

It was a typical campaign week, full to the brim. Both Becky and Mrs. Caulkins were hard put to keep up with the energetic Barbara. "It was exhausting," said Becky, who was in her twenties at the time. "She had a whole lot more energy than I did."

The events in Michigan also were typical of those that Barbara attended, especially in the first year of the campaign. "Early on, I'd say we met in people's houses mostly," Becky said, usually with no more than fifty people attending.

The two of them traveled to every state except Alaska, but spent a disproportionate amount of their time in Iowa because George was trying hard to win the first-in-the-nation caucuses there so he would stand out in the field of Republican candidates. "I think she went to all ninety-nine of Iowa's counties before the caucus," Becky said. "She spent a lot of time."

She recalled one harrowing day in Iowa where she and Barbara were riding on a single-engine private plane in terrible weather with a pilot who appeared to be in his eighties. The plane landed safely, but, said Becky, "I'm sure that was the last time we ever went on a single-engine plane."

Another time, in the dead of the frigid Iowa winter, "we were staying at a hotel in an itty, bitty tiny town and the locks to the car were frozen when we tried to leave the next morning. The girl who was driving us had to get a hair dryer and melt them."

Shortly before the all-important Iowa caucus, when the entire family was campaigning at full tilt, Barbara and George met by accident in Chicago.

"Mrs. Bush and I were changing planes in Chicago," Becky said. "We didn't realize it but so were Mr. Bush and

David Bates," his personal assistant. "We were literally carrying all our bags, a lot of them, and we looked up and here come Mr. Bush and David. It was the first time they had seen each other in a week."

The Bushes kissed, but it was a brief encounter. "We were off to catch another flight and so were they," Becky said. "We didn't have any idea we were going to run into each other."

Chance meetings and occasional weekends were the only times the Bushes were together for most of a year. The grueling schedule sometimes got Barbara down, but she wanted to prove—to herself, her children, and her husband—that she could make a substantial contribution to the campaign.

"The majority of the time during the first presidential campaign, they were separate," Becky said. "Both of us would get a little frustrated being out on the road so long. She missed not only Mr. Bush, but her kids. But she wanted to give it one hundred percent and she did."

The two women ate where they could—at receptions, luncheons, or even in the car, and Barbara was introduced to new cultural experiences along the way.

"She had never been to McDonald's until she met me," Becky said.

To her delight, Becky found Barbara to have a sunny temperament. "I consider her to be one of the genuinely nicest people I've ever known," she said. "Any time she had a sharp tongue she was always right. . . . She never was upset about anything she didn't have a reason to be."

Occasionally things would go awry. Becky recalled a fairly large event—a couple of hundred people—where Barbara was doing her slide show. She narrated and Becky flipped the slides—too fast, as it turned out.

"She said later she could tell when I wasn't paying attention," Becky said. "I would hit the button faster to hurry her along. By that time, I knew every word she was going to say."

Shirley Pettis, who had just retired from Congress when George Bush began his presidential campaign, worked for him in California and she invited Barbara to speak.

"She had by then found her own self, speaking wise," Mrs. Pettis said. "I got an enthusiastic group of former constituents, quite a few of them, about five hundred invitations, to join me for a brunch at the San Bernardino County museum, headlined Bar Bush with her pictures from China. She came out and stayed with me at Loma Linda. The event was very well attended."

When Barbara saw the large audience, her first thought was that the candidate himself should be on hand. "She said, 'Oh my soul, George should be here,' " Mrs. Pettis recalled.

But as it turned out the rally was a success even without the candidate, in part because Barbara and Shirley shared with the audience the warm and teasing relationship they had had as neighbors in Washington.

"We had fun," Mrs. Pettis recalled.

Barbara stuck with her slide show on China for about a year, then decided she could speak on her own without it. She worked out a basic speech with George Bush as the focus, talking about their family life, his accomplishments, and his goals.

Janet Steiger remembers Barbara giving that speech to a college audience in Beloit, Wisconsin, and was impressed that she could hold the attention of college kids at a political rally.

"She has the amazing ability to create rapport no matter what the generation," Mrs. Steiger said. "I was struck by that because that [college] generation is always a generation to and of itself."

When Barbara looks back on the 1980 campaign, she remembers it fondly, not least because she and her children developed new relationships while working to elect George Bush president.

"I liked it for a lot of reasons, not the end result, but I liked the campaigning," she said. "I felt I was really helping

George. I probably lost votes by the hundreds, but I thought I was helping. The children and I all got much closer to each other and to George. Every one of them did their part, and it's true that they now treat me as an adult for the first time."

She said that Doro probably grew the most during the campaign. "She was too shy to speak and . . . [her father] told her nobody wanted her if she didn't have a talent. So she went nine straight months to Katherine Gibbs [secretarial school] and put herself in his office."

The end result, she said, was that "I think they thought that I did a pretty good job campaigning and I know I thought they did."

When the actual political contests started in late 1979 and early 1980, it appeared that their efforts would pay off. George Bush won a straw poll—no delegates but good publicity—in Maine in November, and the victory was seen as an upset because other Republican candidates had put more time into the state than Bush had. Then, on January 21, 1980, he won the Iowa caucuses, coming in two percentage points ahead of Ronald Reagan.

That victory pulled him out of the pack of candidates and marked him as the chief contender against Ronald Reagan, who had established his credentials as front-runner early on based on the strong race he had run against Gerald Ford four years earlier.

Suddenly national reporters and TV crews were paying close attention to the campaign, seeing a potentially successful challenge to Reagan. The whole Bush family was elated, and George exulted that he had the "Big Mo," or the necessary momentum to keep him ahead of his rivals.

Barbara, riding a plane out of Iowa after the caucus vote, was working on her needlepoint when *Detroit News* reporter Jerald terHorst asked what she was doing. "That's interesting," he said. "It looks like a seat cover."

Barbara replied, "It's for George and I'm leaving the needle in it. He's got to keep moving."[1]

The next major contest was the New Hampshire primary,

which had marked the end of many a political campaign over the years. What is best remembered from that contest was a remark that Reagan, with his great sense of theater, made at Bush's expense before an important audience.

The incident occurred at a debate that had been arranged by the *Nashua Telegraph* between the two GOP front-runners, Reagan and Bush, three days before the February 26 vote. Reagan's campaign had agreed to finance the event. When other Republican candidates asked if they could take part, Reagan was agreeable to the idea. Bush was not.

When Reagan got on stage, it was clear the audience wanted all the candidates to take part in the debate. Reagan took the microphone to say he agreed. John Breen, editor of the *Nashua Telegraph,* was angered at this change of plans and told a technician to turn Reagan's microphone off.

Reagan replied, "I paid for this microphone, Mr. Green."

Although Reagan got Breen's name wrong, he won his point and the whole evening to boot. The other candidates were kept out of the debate as Bush wanted, but what people remembered was how Reagan had upstaged his opponent.

Reagan won New Hampshire with an impressive 50 percent of the vote. Bush was second with 23 percent.

George Bush went on to win other primaries—in Puerto Rico, Massachusetts, his home state of Connecticut, Pennsylvania, and Washington, D.C. He also won the high-profile Michigan primary in May. But Reagan had won so many more contests by that time that it was clear he would have enough delegates to claim the Republican presidential nomination at the party's convention in July.

Bush, finding he no longer could get many substantial financial contributions in the face of the likely Reagan victory, dropped out of the race on May 26 and said he would support Reagan at the convention and in the fall election.

There is "a widespread perception that the campaign is over," Bush said at this time. "As a result it has become increasingly difficult to raise the funds needed to mount successful campaigns in the remaining major primary states of

New Jersey, Ohio, and California. It has also become clear that no matter how well I might do in New Jersey and Ohio a week from tomorrow, the results in those states would not turn this race around."

He made the announcement at his home base in Houston. Barbara, standing at his side, held on to the shoulders of her four-year-old grandson George P. and blinked back tears. But George was dry-eyed and, in typical fashion, he had a party later in the day for members of the press who had been traveling with him.

Despite George's upbeat demeanor, the next two months were uncomfortable for Barbara. She knew she had to go to the GOP convention in Detroit and put on a happy face. But her heart was not in it. Two years of campaigning had left her wanting George to have the top prize. "When we went to Detroit, my idea was to do the right thing and get it over with," she said years later.

With Reagan certain to get the GOP presidential nomination, the only mystery at the convention was who he would choose as a running mate. George knew he was a possibility, but any hopes he might have had appeared to die when word spread among the delegates that Reagan was talking with former President Gerald Ford about the number-two spot. By Wednesday night of convention week, it appeared to be a done deal.

Bush was sitting with Barbara, son Marvin, and family friends in the Pontchartrain Hotel when the phone rang at 11:37 P.M. James Baker, who had managed the Bush campaign, picked it up and heard Ronald Reagan's voice on the other end.

Quickly Baker hustled everyone out of the room except for Barbara, Marvin, and convention aide Dean Burch. He then handed the phone to George Bush.

Minutes later Bush emerged from the hotel room to tell reporters that "out of a clear blue sky" Reagan had asked him to run as vice president on the Republican ticket.

"I was surprised," he said. "I of course was very pleased. I told him I would work work work for his election."

Bush later told reporters that he had been so sure Ford would get the nod that he had warned his sons he did not want to see "you guys grumping around here or down or something because something that nobody owed us didn't come to us." But he also tried to instill a little pride in them despite what he expected to be another loss. "Look, we've got twenty-four hours," he told them, "and by gosh, we're going to do this thing with a certain feeling and a certain style and then we'll figure out what to do."[2]

Barbara confessed that "a little competitive spirit" rose up in her during the week, and she was delighted when George won the competition for the number-two spot. "It's funny, everybody makes fun of the job, but everybody I knew there wanted it," she said.

George's new prominence also elevated Barbara into the spotlight. Despite her years of campaigning, she wasn't totally prepared for it. At her first news conference at the convention, she was asked her position on the Equal Rights Amendment, which she had supported in previous years but which Reagan opposed.

"I'm campaigning on the Republican platform," she said. Asked how that squared with her previous position, she simply turned away with a smile.

She knew right away that her performance had been subpar, and she told a reporter later in the day, "I think I answered that question very badly. If I had another shot at answering that question, I would say, 'Do you have any idea, really, of how I feel about abortion and ERA? Because I'm not going to tell you. I'm not running for public office, George Bush is.' "[3]

She added, "I'm not a wave maker. I do not agree with my husband on everything and I'm not going to tell you if I don't agree. Because I am going to tell George Bush how I feel. Upstairs."

Her other answers had a similar defensive, snippy quality to them.

Did she regret dropping out of Smith College? If she had regretted it, she replied, she would have done something about it.

Did she miss having her own career? She had lectured on China, she answered, but she found being a wife and mother more fulfilling.

"I've always been a part of George Bush's life," she said. "He is a sharer. The role of a wife is to be supportive, and I've been very happy these thirty-five years. So don't rock my boat."

As she got into the fall campaign, however, traveling an average of six days a week, Barbara became more accustomed to the spotlight and her humor and natural savvy returned.

By October, for instance, she had a better answer on the Equal Rights Amendment. While she supported it, she said, she had no problem with Reagan opposing it. "I feel my president should be solving problems—economy, foreign affairs, getting a strong, inventive energy program, and strengthening our intelligence service and our defense," she said. "If you want to see ERA passed, you should elect congressmen who feel that way because the president should be giving leadership in these fields that are in crisis."

She took a complimentary, teasing attitude toward the Reagan campaign, saying she had told his aides that if they had let people know earlier about Reagan's "decency, his sensitivity, his caring for people . . . we wouldn't have gotten so far in the primaries."

Regarding Nancy Reagan, she had nothing but praise. She even managed to say something nice about Nancy's strained relationship with her children. "I think the way to judge a mother is by her children," Barbara said. "The thing I like about her children is their independence—which is the best thing you can give your children. They are the four most different children I have ever met but they have one thing in common. They say their father listens to them and they are very supportive of him."[4]

Despite the many compliments she paid to Nancy, Barbara may have realized early on that they would never be close. "We're not going to be able to have hobbies together," she said. "I jog and she rides; she probably would rather die than jog and I put riding up to the top of my rather-die list."

She also acknowledged that campaigning as the wife of the vice presidential candidate instead of the presidential candidate took some adjusting.

"You step back if you're the wife of the man running for vice president," she said. "You want to help as much as you can, but it's a whole different role."[5]

While she refrained from criticizing either Rosalynn Carter or Joan Mondale, wives of the Democratic opposition, Barbara did use Rosalynn to get in a dig at Jimmy Carter, saying Rosalynn must love her husband "a whole bunch because I would have been scared to death to go to a city where they had forty percent unemployment and have to tell them things are getting better."

The voters agreed with Barbara. In the fall election, the Reagan-Bush ticket won an overwhelming victory, receiving 489 electoral votes while Jimmy Carter and Walter Mondale received just 49. She and George and all their children watched the results in a Houston hotel. "We didn't imagine a sweep like this," George said.

The next day George and Barbara flew to Los Angeles to join the Reagans in a victory celebration. They would spend the next eight years in the shadow of the presidential couple. But as it turned out, Barbara didn't mind at all.

Second Lady of the Land

*I*n January 1981 George and Barbara moved into the thirty-three-room vice presidential residence on Massachusetts Avenue in northwest Washington. It would be their home for eight years, the longest they had stayed in one place since they were married.

Barbara found the mansion, built in 1893, spacious and in fairly good shape, since both of the last two vice presidential families—the Rockefellers and the Mondales—had done redecorating. Nevertheless, Bush family friends raised $187,000 for work that George and Barbara wanted done.

The pillared house, set among gently sloping lawns and wooded hills, had a porte-cochere entrance, a broad veranda, and plenty of grounds for planting a garden, jogging, tennis, and walking the cocker spaniel, C. Fred.

Barbara replaced Joan Mondale's abstract paintings with Oriental art. Over an elegant Chinese bureau, she displayed a painting by E. Martin Hennings of two Indians on horseback passing under a gold-leafed tree. She also stretched, framed, and hung two intricately embroidered gold and azure Mandarin Chinese jackets.

She borrowed impressionist art from the Corcoran and

National Galleries in Washington and an Audubon print from the Houston Museum of Art. She put out myriad pictures of the Bush clan and filled the house with flowers. The living-room wallpaper, a sunny yellow floral pattern, added to the bright, airy look.

As they always had before, the Bushes began entertaining immediately, even before Barbara had all her decorating done.

"George wants instant moving," she said. "When we moved to Houston, he had invited the King of Jordan for dinner before we even had a house."

In their first months in the vice presidential house, the Bushes gave a small party for President and Nancy Reagan, a dinner for six, a bash for old Washington friends who had helped house the 150 Bush family members during the inauguration, a party for staff members, and more. A household staff of six helped with the preparations, but Barbara had a dishwasher installed on the first floor of the house so she could entertain her friends without much help from the chefs in the basement kitchen.

Aside from entertaining at home, Barbara had a busy schedule, full of minor but politically necessary public appearances. She visited charities, welcomed Texas students visiting the Capitol, met with Republican groups—mayors, governors, fund-raisers, and wives—and was regularly at George Bush's side for public dinners and speeches.

Her duties, long established by Washington protocol, were an odd mixture. They included riding in a crane to afix a starburst ornament at the top of the national Christmas tree and leading a weekly craft session for Senate wives.

Although most of the nation's attention was focused on the new president, Ronald Reagan, and his wife, Nancy, Barbara drew some notice as well. She received a lot of letters, most of them supportive, but many also wanting to know why she didn't dye her hair.

"When we first got into office, someone wrote and said,

'Dear Mrs. Bush: This is a youthful administration. The vice president looks young. Mrs. Reagan looks young. Why don't you?' " Barbara said. "I wrote back, 'I'm doing the best I can. And besides, I'm the youngest of all those people.' "[1]

As the letters about her hair continued to pour in, she began sending back a standard, humorous, answer: "I said, 'Please forget about my hair. Think about my wonderful mind.' "

She also found, much to her annoyance, that when she made public appearances, people were aware of her busy schedule and often asked if her feet hurt.

"I want to put my mind and my soul into what I do and I'm bored with the hair," she said. "Feet and hair are boring. Who's interested in feet? When you go someplace, people ask if your feet hurt. If they did, I wouldn't tell them!"[2]

Always a high-energy person, Barbara had no problem meeting the demands of the vice president's office. Raising five children, moving dozens of times, and campaigning for almost two years had prepared her well.

"I am now physically and mentally stronger than I was twenty years ago," she said.

Her day started at 6 or 6:30 A.M. with coffee and the newspapers in bed. She and George took turns getting the coffee.

By 7 A.M. she was doing her exercises, sometimes using George's new running machine while she watched the morning news shows on television.

Old friends found she was still an old friend.

"Whatever seems to happen to political wives didn't happen to her," said tennis partner Ellen Sulzberger Straus. "When you live in Washington, you notice that as these people get to the top they get stuffier and stuffier. That just isn't the case with Barbara. She doesn't take herself too seriously. There is no phoniness about her."[3]

Longtime friend Andy Stewart was surprised to find that Barbara had planned a large birthday party for her in cahoots with other members of the Stewart family.

"I was completely surprised," Mrs. Stewart said. "My

daughter and some relatives came from out of town. It was so thoughtful because my husband had died just a year before. It was a wonderful sit-down luncheon, maybe sixty people. I was so overwhelmed, I walked right in the door and didn't recognize my own daughter."

The thrifty habits Barbara had developed as a young wife at Yale and in West Texas stayed with her, even as her husband rose in prominence. While Bush was in Congress she had taken an automobile mechanics class and thereafter performed some of the repairs on the family cars herself. She also had picked up a little knowledge about electrical wiring, as a Washington contractor discovered when he got a call one day from the vice president's wife. She was at Marvin's house trying to rig the wiring when she ran into a problem.

"Here was the wife of the vice president using her own tools stripping wires and fooling around with switches to save some money," said the contractor. "It was just like her, but I sent my electrician over."[4]

Barbara still made jokes, and her repertoire had expanded to the rich and famous. After Prince Charles had dinner at the vice presidential mansion, she remarked that having him as her dinner companion was "like sitting next to one of my four sons only he's better dressed and more polite."

Noting that a highly visible job of vice presidents in recent years has been to attend funerals of foreign dignitaries, Barbara quoted family friend James Baker saying of George Bush "You die, he'll fly."

She didn't always follow protocol. She noticed that the rigid dictates of seating in official Washington often left a visiting foreign official sitting next to the same person for three dinners in a row. So when the party was at her house, she changed the seating; that way, everyone would have someone new to talk with.

And although an honored male guest at the vice president's house would normally sit at Barbara's table, that didn't always happen with Barbara in charge.

"This poor man didn't come to the United States to sit

next to me," she said. "So I'll try to put him at the table with George so they can talk. I always make it clear that this is not the vice president's idea and they're very nice about it."

She and George went to endless numbers of dinner parties themselves and found a way to amuse themselves even when the speeches were long and dull and the food close to inedible.

"Sometimes, well, almost all the time, there'll be an after-dinner speaker who reminds us of something funny," she said. "I look across at George and get laughing 'cause he knows what I'm thinking and I know exactly how it's going to grab him." She adds diplomatically, "Of course, I hope other people laugh at us, too."[5]

She certainly laughed at her own mistakes. When the Archbishop of Canturbury visited Washington with his primates, they dressed in traditional purple and red. Barbara, forgetting the church's colors, said, "I got up in the morning and thought, 'It's still cool enough to wear my purple dress and red coat'—so did they, all of them."

During a visit to Ghana, her duties included watching a man bite the head off a chicken. "I made up my mind that no matter what he did I wouldn't react," she said. "And I didn't react. But people around me were dropping like flies."

Barbara had always bought her own clothes right off the racks in retail stores as most people do, but she found as the vice president's wife, she couldn't go shopping without causing a commotion. The Secret Service had to go along and other shoppers would come up and greet her. She began to have her clothes made, but her taste was not extravagant and she never attracted the kind of attention Nancy Reagan did with her designer dresses.

"I spend time and effort but no one thinks of me as well dressed," Barbara joked. "It takes a lot of strain off you."

For the same reasons she no longer shopped in public, Barbara couldn't spontaneously visit her children or old friends in other cities, a curb on her freedom that she learned to live with but sometimes regretted.

"I can't just hop on a plane and fly to see my new grandson in Texas," she said. "The taxpayers would have to pay for the Secret Service agents who would have to go with me."[6]

Barbara did travel extensively, both with George and on her own, to a total of sixty-eight countries while he was vice president. She met almost all the world leaders. "Not that they know me, but I knew them," she said.

Despite her busy schedule, she remained relatively low profile. She joked that a Swedish embassy reception given in honor of her and George was an exercise in humiliation.

"Usually you don't hear anything in a receiving line but this night I heard three things," she said. "One person gave me a quizzical look and said, 'Who are you?' Another person looked thrilled, recognition flooding her face and said, 'Well, hello Mrs. Schultz' [thinking Barbara was Helena Schultz, wife of Secretary of State George Schultz]. And the one I really loved was a darling man who got to me, warmly clasped my hand in both of his and said, 'Welcome to our country.' "[7]

Barbara loved the privacy that the woodsy grounds of the vice presidential mansion provided and professed sympathy for Nancy Reagan in the much more public White House.

"I feel so lucky being here," she said. "I think how awful it must be for Nancy Reagan not being able to walk around the lawn, having strangers wandering through the downstairs rooms all morning."

There were times, however, when her own privacy was interrupted. Early one morning when Soviet Foreign Minister Eduard Shevardnadze was to have breakfast at the vice presidential house, Barbara put on her bathrobe and started to take her dog for a brief walk outdoors. She was stopped short by a Secret Service agent, who warned her the grounds were full of photographers awaiting Shevardnadze's arrival. So she sneaked back into the house, went up to her dressing room—and found the photographers directly below the window. "I had to crawl to my closet to get my clothes," she said.

While Barbara was often humorous in public, she seldom spoke out on the major issues of the day, except in her chosen fields of illiteracy, home, and family. Even so, she soon learned that her husband's new position put her much in demand. "I'm finding lots of groups that might not be too hot to hear you as just Barbara Bush want you as a speaker because your husband is vice president," she said.

She had long been a supporter of a proposed constitutional amendment to guarantee equal rights to women, but she also felt strongly that families, especially women, needed to pay closer attention to their children.

"I don't think men and women should have children and not take responsibility," she said in 1984. "Men are going to have to take a lot more responsibility. They will have to do more as their share. But women are also going to have to learn that they have to have priorities, that they have to make choices, and that they can't have everything. You can't, in my opinion, be a bank president and a full-time mother."

Realizing many women must work to help support a family—her own daughter would divorce and go to work a few years later—Barbara said she felt it was so important to have someone home with a child for the first four or five years that families should be willing to make sacrifices to ensure full-time parental care.

Later she would refine and change some of these views. Her support for the Equal Rights Amendment eventually faded when it became clear that it didn't have enough support in the states to win. But she remained friendly to those who were working for the ERA.

During the inaugural parade in January 1985, Barbara and George were riding with the Reagans when they passed a group of women holding up signs in support of the amendment. Neither the Reagans nor George Bush acknowledged the group but Barbara turned, smiled, and held up her fingers in a victory sign, according to Molly Yard, then president of the National Organization for Women, who was among the sign-holders.

Throughout the 1984 reelection campaign, however, Barbara defended Ronald Reagan's record on women, noting that he had appointed Sandra Day O'Connor to the Supreme Court and had two women in his Cabinet. She argued that "women's issues" were the same ones that concerned men.

"I'm not as convinced any more that the Equal Rights Amendment is half as important as seeing that women get equal pay for equal work, pension plans, deductions for child care, and seeing that husbands who are delinquent in child support are made to make payments," she said.

"The main thing for women is that we have peace, that we have a strong economy, that we get inflation down, that people can buy a home and get jobs," she said. "Reagan has done a wonderful job on these things and that should count for women."

Because the Democratic candidate, Vice President Walter Mondale, had chosen Congresswoman Geraldine Ferraro as his running mate, Barbara was frequently asked what she thought of a woman as vice president.

In a campaign speech in March 1984 to the National Federation of Republican Women she said, "Just this morning two newscasters were saying that the only qualified women for vice president were Republicans. That's true. But we already have a vice president we like very much."

She was always ready to defend her husband and took any slights to him personally, a trait that Bush appreciated with a certain wariness.

"She'll go to bat for me, sometimes more than I'm inclined to myself," he said. "I'm glad to have her defend me. I'd rather have her on my side than not."

At the Republican convention that August in Dallas, Barbara was asked again if she thought a woman could be a good vice president. By that time she had a different answer.

"In my opinion, the vice president should be qualified to be president," she replied. "So the question should be, 'What do you think of a woman for president?' And I plan to vote for one surely before I die—and she will be a Republican."

Was Mrs. Ferraro an asset to Mondale?

"Yes," Barbara said carefully. "But you have to remember we're saying Mondale and I don't know if she would be to anyone—but certainly to Vice President Mondale."

Later in the campaign, however, Barbara got angry at Geraldine Ferraro and had an outburst that she came to regret.

The incident occurred in early October as she was traveling on *Air Force Two* to a Columbus Day parade in New York. She walked back to talk with reporters, and the discussion turned to accusations made by Mondale and Ferraro that rich people like the Bushes were out of touch with the needs of everyday Americans.

Barbara had gotten increasingly annoyed at the suggestion, since many Democrats were just as rich as the Bushes. Talking to the reporters, she blurted out that Mrs. Ferraro had more money than the Bushes and went on to describe her as a "four million dollar—I can't say it but it rhymes with rich."

Within hours, the story was being broadcast all over the country and Barbara realized she had made a mistake. She quickly called Geraldine Ferraro to apologize and said publicly that she regretted the remark.

Privately she cried and cried, knowing that such a remark had been out of line. "It hurt me a whole bunch," she said later.

Geraldine Ferraro accepted the apology but her mother, Antonetta, was indignant at the insult. "I thought it was terrible," she told reporters. "I would not put myself in her category. So she apologized. Empty words."

Barbara was afraid her remark would hurt the campaign, and she was careful to temper her future remarks about Mrs. Ferraro.

As it turned out, her slip-up had little, if any, effect. Reagan and Bush won an overwhelming victory in the election a month later. They carried every state except Mondale's own, Minnesota, and the District of Columbia.

The inaugural in January 1985 was a flashy one, full of minks, limousines, big diamonds, showy shoes, and other signs of money. Having recovered from the deep recession of 1981–82, the economy was hot, Wall Street was knee-deep in multibillion-dollar deals, and the mood in the country was one of celebration and extravagance.

Barbara took part in the festivities with pleasure, but without much extravagance, careful as usual to leave the spotlight on Nancy Reagan and enjoy herself in the shadows.

For the inaugural, she ordered a $6,000 white wool coat with jewel buttons and a $10,000 white mink blouson jacket. Both were modest compared with the $100,000 furs wrapped around many of the inaugural guests.

Barbara and George had their own inaugural party one night before the more glitzy affair held for the Reagans. Frank Sinatra had been scheduled as emcee, but since he was to star at the Reagan gala, he turned his duties over to Merv Griffin, who joked to the Bushes, "Obviously, you couldn't get tickets to the Super Bowl either."

The Bushes didn't seem to mind. Although the 6,000-seat Washington Convention Center was not full for the vice presidential tribute, both Barbara and George looked to be enjoying themselves.

It was typical of the political life the Bushes led as number-two couple. They were seldom in the news or more than a sideline at the major events of the day. Barbara would say later that she "got away with murder" during the vice presidential years. Since few people noticed what she did, she wasn't under the intense pressure that goes with being First Lady, although Barbara did make the list of the "Ten Best Mannered Americans." She was chosen as most charming.

Nancy Reagan wasn't above snubbing Barbara, despite Barbara's protests that the relationship was a friendly one. The insult was especially apparent when Mikhail and Raisa Gorbachev visited Washington in 1987. Both Washington and Moscow realized from previous meetings that Nancy and Raisa didn't get along well, and the Soviets indicated they would like Barbara Bush to accompany Raisa to the National Gallery of Art.

But word came back quickly from the White House. "That was not to be encouraged," Bush aide Craig Fuller said. "It was made clear that this would not be looked upon favorably." Nancy made sure she would not be upstaged by Barbara.

Barbara has said repeatedly that she hated comparisons between Nancy and herself, and she did what she could to cool speculation that the two couples were not friends. Nevertheless, except for official functions where they had to be together, the Reagans and the Bushes went their separate ways.

During her second four years in the vice presidential mansion, Barbara calculated how she allocated her days—"I spend fifty percent of my time doing charitable work and twenty-five percent on organizational things like running the house," she said. "Maybe fifteen percent on my husband and children and maybe ten percent on myself, exercising and playing tennis."

Her charitable work included a substantial amount of entertaining. Her style was much the same as it had always been.

"It's not changed all that much," said longtime friend Jessica Catto. "They've always been gracious but informal and they had, as I remember, their friends and people in government, the same kind of mix they have now."

The Cattos usually visited the vice presidential house with a small group of old Bush friends, and it was inevitably an early evening. "We might go to a Chinese restaurant, or something like that," she said. "They're pretty early retirers. The party would end by ten," at the latest.

For large groups, Barbara liked to do afternoon parties, especially teas. In the spring of 1986, *McCall's* magazine was on hand for a tea at the vice presidential mansion in honor of a joint literacy campaign by ABC and the Public Broadcasting Corporation.

While Mrs. Bush talked with the reporter, she drank a cup of tea with a lemon slice studded with cloves.

She said she usually used Lenox china with the vice presidential seal for large parties, but for small, more personal gatherings where breakage is less likely, she preferred her own Tiffany pattern.

The dining-room table, a ten-foot-long mahogany, was bare to show off the polished wood. A floral arrangement in the center was surrounded by china and silver platters filled with tea sandwiches and cookies arranged in concentric circles over lace paper doilies. The sandwiches included watercress, smoked salmon, chicken and tuna eclairs, tomatoes stuffed with cream cheese and dill, and one hot hors d'oeuvre—cheese puffs. In addition, there were brownies, lace cookies, and pecan tartlets.

At both ends of the table were silver tea services and gold-rimmed cups and saucers marked with the vice presidential seal. Glasses of white wine sat on a tray on a sideboard.

Barbara said that while she consulted the chef and other staff members about decorations, she didn't worry if the final arrangements were not what she would have chosen.

At the tea party, for example, the dining room had a number of vases filled with flowers in addition to the bouquet at center table. "Personally I prefer one strong floral arrangement to a jungle like this," Barbara said. "But I'm not going to get disturbed about that. It's not essential to the success of the party."

She recalled that when Margaret Thatcher visited the vice presidential mansion, the navy stewards for some reason changed the pastel icing on the petits fours to orange, purple, and red, much to Barbara's surprise.

"I just laughed," she said. "It wasn't that important. If you have a good time yourself, others will."

Here are the recipes that Barbara gave to *McCall's,* including some from the tea party.[8]

CHEESE PUFFS

12 slices white bread
One-half pound American cheese, grated
One small onion, grated
Dash of white pepper
One-half cup mayonnaise

Preheat oven to 200 degrees Fahrenheit. Cut bread into one-and-one-half- to one-and-three-quarters-inch rounds, four per slice. Place bread rounds on baking sheets. Bake 10 minutes.

Meanwhile, combine American cheese, onion, pepper and mayonnaise. Remove bread rounds to wire rack. Increase oven temperature to 325 degrees Fahrenheit. Spread a teaspoonful of cheese mixture on each bread round; place on lightly greased baking sheets. Bake five minutes. Makes four dozen cheese puffs.

CHICKEN SALAD ECLAIRS

One-half cup shortening
Dash of salt
One cup boiling water
One cup sifted all-purpose flour
Three eggs
Chicken salad, recipe below

In medium saucepan, combine shortening, salt and boiling water. Cook over medium heat until mixture comes to a boil and shortening is melted. Lower heat and add flour all at once. Cook, stirring, until mixture leaves the side of the pan and forms a ball. Remove from heat. Beat in eggs, one at a time, beating well after each addition.

Preheat oven to 425 degrees Fahrenheit. Using a pastry bag, drop eclairs onto ungreased baking sheet, about one inch apart, using about one teaspoon of dough for each. Bake fifteen minutes. Cool on wire rack.

Split in half to fill. Spoon about one teaspoonful of chicken salad into each eclair. Replace tops. Makes four dozen.

CHICKEN SALAD

One cooked whole breast of chicken, boned, skinned, and diced
One celery stalk, diced
Two tablespoons mayonnaise

In medium bowl, combine all ingredients and blend well. If necessary, add enough additional mayonnaise to hold mixture together.

WATERCRESS TEA SANDWICHES

One eight-ounce package cream cheese
One teaspoon fresh dill, chopped
Two tablespoons parsley, chopped
10 slices white bread, crusts removed, and flattened with a rolling pin
Watercress sprigs

Combine cream cheese, dill and chopped parsley. Cut bread slices in quarters. Spread the cream cheese combination on top; insert a sprig of watercress; roll up well, making sure that a bit of watercress peeks through. Makes forty sandwiches.

VICE PRESIDENT'S HOUSE
OATMEAL-LACE COOKIES

One-half cup all-purpose
    flour
One-fourth teaspoon baking
    powder
One-half cup sugar
One-half cup rolled oats

Two tablespoons
    heavy cream
One-third cup melted
    butter
Two tablespoons
    white corn syrup
One teaspoon vanilla
    extract

Preheat oven to 375 degrees Fahrenheit. Sift together flour, baking powder and sugar. Add oats, cream, butter, corn syrup and vanilla. Mix until well blended. Drop by slightly heaped quarter teaspoonfuls onto a greased cookie sheet, allowing four inches between each. Bake approximately six minutes or until lightly browned. Check after four minutes. Let stand a few minutes before removing from pan. Makes four dozen cookies.

MRS. BUSH'S HONEY BUNCHES

Three cups quick-cooking rolled oats
Two cups flaked coconut
One cup all-purpose flour
One and one-half cups firmly packed
    brown sugar
One cup unsalted butter
One-third cup honey

Preheat oven to 350 degrees Fahrenheit. In a large mixing bowl, combine oats, coconut and flour. In a heavy saucepan, combine the remaining ingredients and bring to a boil. Pour over the dry ingredients; blend well. Drop dough by tea-spoonfuls into greased muffin cups or foil baking cups placed on a cookie sheet. Bake twelve to fifteen minutes or until well browned. Cool in pans. Makes about four dozen cookies.

Mrs. Bush's tip: If desired, substitute one cup chopped walnuts and one cup flaked coconut for the two cups coconut.

BUSH FAMILY CHOCOLATE CHIP COOKIES

One cup plus two tablespoons sifted all-purpose flour
One-half teaspoon baking soda
One-half teaspoon salt
One-half cup softened butter
One-third cup granulated sugar
One-third cup firmly packed brown sugar
One egg
One-half teaspoon vanilla extract
One-half tablespoon very hot water
One cup semisweet chocolate pieces

Preheat oven to 375 degrees Fahrenheit. Sift to-gether the flour, baking soda and salt. Combine the butter and sugars with the egg. Beat until creamy. Add the dry ingredients to the butter mixture. Mix thoroughly. Add the vanilla and the hot water. Stir in the chocolate pieces. Drop by well-rounded half teaspoonfuls onto a greased cookie sheet. Bake ten to twelve minutes. Makes three dozen cookies.

PECAN TARTLETS

One three-ounce package
  cream cheese
One cup all-purpose flour
One-half cup plus one
  tablespoon unsalted
  butter
One egg

Three-fourths cup
  brown sugar
One teaspoon vanilla
  extract
Dash of salt
Coarsely chopped
  pecans

Preheat oven to 375 degrees Fahrenheit. Combine the cream cheese, flour and one-half cup butter to make a dough. Taking about a teaspoon of dough at a time, press into the tiniest muffin molds. Combine the egg, one tablespoon butter, the brown sugar, vanilla and salt. Fill each shell with a teaspoonful or so of the filling. Sprinkle the tops with pecans. Bake ten to fifteen minutes. Makes four dozen tartlets.

BUSH FAMILY ICED TEA

One gallon water
Seven tea bags
Four sprigs fresh mint leaves
Juice of three lemons
One six-ounce can frozen orange juice concentrate
One-third cup superfine sugar

Boil the water. Add tea bags and mint leaves. Remove from heat; let steep fifteen minutes. Remove the tea bags and mint leaves. Add lemon juice, orange juice and sugar. Refrigerate until serving time. Makes twelve servings.

9

White House Here
We Come

*E*arly in George Bush's 1988
presidential campaign, he
made a stop in San Antonio, Texas. A local news photographer, trying to get a good picture of the candidate, was
annoyed to find a woman in the way.

"Will the woman in the red dress please get out of the
picture?" he shouted.

Barbara Bush looked around for the woman, then realized
with a start that the photographer was talking about her.
After eight years as the vice president's wife, she was still just
"the woman in the red dress" to millions of Americans.

During the long months of the campaign, however, she
began to shed her anonymity. Moving out from under
Nancy Reagan's shadow, Barbara would become a woman
recognized wherever she went, a change she anticipated with
mixed feelings. Being in the spotlight certainly had a downside, as she already knew.

The previous summer had brought an ugly reminder of
what can happen to people in public life, especially as they
move higher up the political ladder and go after jobs for

which there is cutthroat competition. Several months before
Bush had formally announced his candidacy in October 1987,
old rumors began circulating through Washington linking
him romantically with a former female staff member. Both
Newsweek magazine and *U.S. News and World Report* printed
the rumors, along with denials from Bush and his son George
that an affair had occurred.

Barbara was hurt and angry. "How do you defend against
something that didn't happen?" she said. "It was a large fat
smear and I didn't like it one bit . . . I hated it for him. I
hated it for us."

Her protective instincts toward George were also sparked
by insinuations that he had played a role in the unsavory
Iran-Contra arms deal. It was, she said, "an example of the
negative tone of the entire campaign.

"The ugliness of politics has been very bad this year, Democrats and Republicans . . . it's been very hurtful and I don't
like that," she said.[1]

Then, in the Iowa caucuses in February 1988, George had
an unexpected and humiliating loss to televangelist Pat Robertson, which led to much speculation about whether he
could win the Republican nomination. Barbara was so dis-
gusted with what was being said that she refused to watch
television news or read newspapers for a while.

"George doesn't like me to say it because it makes you
sound like a nincompoop when you say you don't follow the
news," she said. "But . . . it's just hard to go out and campaign for twelve hours when you're hearing such depressing
things."

As in previous campaigns, the question of her white hair
and wrinkled face came up frequently, but this time in more
brutal form. NBC's Jane Pauley told Barbara on camera that
people were saying "Your husband is a man of the eighties
and you're a woman of the forties. What do you say to that?"

Barbara was taken aback, but maintained her composure
enough to answer. Later, however, she admitted that the

question had hurt. "She's lucky I didn't burst into sobbing tears," Barbara said.

As questions about her looks continued, she responded in various ways, sometimes with unconcealed anger, other times with a more temperate answer.

"I'm not going to turn into a glamorous princess," she said shortly before the GOP convention in August. "I'm not going to worry about it. I have plenty of self-confidence, not in how I look but in how I feel and I feel good about my husband, my children, and my life."

At the same time she told reporters she admired the looks of Kitty Dukakis, wife of Democratic presidential candidate Michael Dukakis. "I'd love to look like her if you want to know the truth," she said.

Barbara spent almost as much time on the road campaigning as George did. She frequently used slides when she spoke before a group, many of them designed to show George Bush as a leader and happy family man. The audience favorite was a snapshot of George and Barbara in bed early one morning at their summer house in Kennebunkport, Maine, with grandchildren bouncing around them and playing on the floor. Barbara looked alert, but George still appeared sleepy.

There also were slides of George with world leaders, George at the Berlin Wall, and George at the Wailing Wall. Sometimes there was a videotape of George describing Barbara's life, with an emphasis on the humorous.

One anecdote was set in a bookstore, where Barbara was signing copies of *C. Fred's Story,* the first book she wrote about the family cocker spaniel.

"Where's C. Fred?" Bush quoted a woman who came into the store saying. When told that the dog was home in Washington, the woman was indignant. "You mean I came here for nothing," she said.

Barbara used this self-deprecating humor to great effect, soon becoming a favorite with campaign audiences. She also revealed little bits of family trivia that added to the enjoyment.

"George Bush sleeps with two girls," she deadpanned, pausing for effect. "Millie and me"—a reference to the springer spaniel the Bushes got after C. Fred died.

Although Barbara generally refused to answer questions on political issues of the day, she occasionally aimed a sting against her husband's opponents for the GOP nomination.

Campaigning in Texas, where Robertson had been showing strength, she was asked whether he was a threat. "We don't need anyone who sees missiles on Cuba when they're not there," she replied, referring to Robertson's unsubstantiated, sensationalist claim that the Soviets had nuclear weapons in Cuba.

But she had learned a lesson from her brush with infamy in the 1984 Ferraro rhymes-with-rich incident. During one campaign trip in 1988, she was steaming about remarks Senator Bob Dole had made questioning whether George would be tough enough as president. Talking with reporters on the campaign plane, Barbara was suddenly aware of George Bush coming up behind her. "I better get back to my seat," she said. "The poet laureate has retired."

Despite having angry feelings toward Bush's opponents, Barbara made clear that if George lost, it wouldn't be the end of the world for her. Having been through two losing Senate races and an unsuccessful presidential campaign with her husband, she knew that life didn't end at the ballot box.

"No matter what happens I'm going to have puppies next year by this time," she told the *Baltimore Sun*. "And I'm going to beg George to take me down the Inland Waterway by boat. I've always wanted to do that. And I wouldn't mind taking a barge trip through the French wine country. And I'd like to go to Baja fishing again. We did that once. And I'm going to dig in my garden, and I'm going to play with my ten grandchildren, and I'm going to read a lot more. I might even write some. I'm going to do a lot of needlepoint. I'm going to walk six miles every day. And I'll play with my friends, while they can still play."

Whatever her real feelings about the campaign, Barbara was able to put on the required happy face for the Republican convention, held in mid-August in New Orleans. She and George and several grandchildren had been in Kennebunkport in early August as usual, but if Barbara had regrets about leaving her cool oceanside estate in Maine for the steamy, crowded streets of New Orleans, she didn't let on.

Both she and Kitty Dukakis had agreed to write daily convention diaries for *USA Today*. Barbara used hers in large part to introduce the wider Bush family to the American public. She started writing from Kennebunkport. By the Sunday of convention week, all the family had departed from the summer home except for Barbara and Jeb's three children. "The four of us are sitting here right now looking at each other thinking, 'Why aren't we there where all the fun is,' " she wrote. She and twelve-year-old George P. shared their jitters, since he was to give the Pledge of Allegiance the following Tuesday at the convention and Barbara had to give a speech.

"There are many pros and cons to being the grandchild of the vice president," Barbara wrote. "Tuesday night will be one of the pros. On the con side: He got into a knock-down, drag-out fight with another boy at camp a few weeks ago out of loyalty to his grandfather."[2]

George P. and his two siblings, the children of Jeb and Columba Bush, were the ones George Bush referred to affectionately during the campaign as "the little brown ones." The phrase offended some people, but the initial buzz was quieted by the Bushes' outraged reaction that anyone would imply that George had demeaned his grandchildren. Americans would learn later that he had an especially close relationship with George P., his first grandchild.

On Monday, the day before the Bushes arrived at the convention, Barbara closed up the Kennebunkport house, doing the kind of homey chores many women could identify with. She said she put fresh sheets on all the beds, emptied vases, bid farewell to her beloved garden, and gave the man who takes care of the grounds in her absence some final instructions. She didn't plan to iron her clothes until she got to New Orleans, but it was the first thing she did when she arrived.

The night before she left for New Orleans, Barbara had dinner with George's eighty-seven-year-old mother and his even older aunt, Margie Clement. "One of the great reasons Mrs. Bush has been a wonderful mother-in-law is that she always pretended her four daughters-in-law were the four most wonderful women she's known," Barbara said. "I've tried to do the same with my daughters-in-law, but I know I'm bossier."[3]

George and Barbara made a grand entrance into New Orleans, arriving in a riverboat filled with their family and friends and the newly chosen vice presidential couple, Dan and Marilyn Quayle.

"I was overcome with emotion," Barbara said. "It sort of hit me that this was really happening."

She said that while George had told her his choice of vice president during the plane trip to New Orleans, she had figured it out the night before by a process of elimination.

"I also think it's a sign of living together for forty-three years," she said. "You think alike."

Wednesday was the first full day of convention for Barbara. She got up at four-thirty in the morning to prepare for a super-full day, including a round of breakfast meetings, each featuring a specific voter group—blacks, Latinos, Jews, and the elderly. At the breakfast with blacks, she ran into an old friend from Houston, former American Football League player Ernie Ladd. "I like to stand next to him," Barbara said. "He makes me feel tiny."

Later in the day she visited a day-care facility that doubled as a meeting place for senior citizens. "What an extraordinary place it is," she said. "The children had a little song for me and showed me their arts and crafts."

She practiced her speech and stood at the podium in the convention center, both to get a feel for it and to combat the nervous sensation that hit her when she thought of addressing the thousands of delegates who would fill the empty seats.

Wednesday night she had dinner with the extended Bush family—sixty-five people in all. "One of the brothers took a poll of all the family members to see who had the grayest hair and he said I won," Barbara reported, adding a typical mother's lament: "Unfortunately, Marvin was runner-up for the family member with the longest hair."

She noted that her daughter-in-law Columba, Jeb's wife, had celebrated her thirty-fifth birthday that day and had also given a seconding speech for George Bush's nomination, first in Spanish, then in English. Columba had just become an American citizen that year, Barbara said, and "I'm bursting with pride."

Thursday, the final day of the convention, was also the most fun for Barbara. Not only did George give a widely admired acceptance speech that night, but she was honored earlier in day at a free-spirited luncheon filled with family and friends.

She woke up at 4:00 A.M. in nervous anticipation, checking her clock every ten minutes to see if it was time to get up. When she rose she washed her hair, ironed a dress, and was ready to appear on the morning news shows by six-fifteen. She joked that on the way to her interviews she saw a newsman she knew sleeping soundly on the floor. "I stopped for a moment and wrote him a note that said, 'I came by to give you an interview. Sorry I missed you.' Then I signed my name and left it on his tummy."

At the luncheon in her honor, sponsored by the National Federation of Republican Women, the highlight was a teasing display of affection between George and Barbara, a response to her earlier complaint that Kitty and Michael Dukakis were simply looking for votes with their lovey-dovey public stance. "I don't like the faking. I don't like the holding hands and all those things," Barbara had said in a TV interview a week earlier.

When George introduced his wife at the luncheon, he told the crowd he had been instructed by his aides to loosen up and "be a little more demonstrative."

"So here we go," he said, "The introduction—with feeling. Come on up, sweetie pie."

Barbara Bush grinned as she moved toward the podium and gave her husband an exaggerated hug. "Thank you very, very much—sweetie," she said. Then, turning to the crowd, she added, "See if he looks at me adoringly—as I looked at him."

The audience was delighted, and there were more tributes to come.

Bush campaign manager Lee Atwater said that Barbara had "an uncommon degree of common sense" and was a buoyant presence on the campaign trail.

"You can't imagine how tough it got out there for six or seven months, trudging around during this so-called Iranian mess," he said. Atwater recalled that when he was depressed and "sitting there looking a little sad, she'd always come up to me and say, 'cheer up jittery jattery.' "

Dorothy Bush LeBlond choked up during a tribute to her mother, saying she was "someone who was always there," and a woman who "stands out like a beacon for those of us searching for real people." She added that Barbara had spent many years "on the front lines of domestic warfare . . . putting up with my four brothers without hazardous duty pay." At that point she was interrupted with a loud boo from one of those brothers.

Barbara, clearly pleased by the happy mood and fond words, told the crowd that she felt like the world's luckiest woman. "Nobody has ever had dearer friends, nobody ever had a greater, more precious family, nobody ever had a better husband," she said.

"You know, today, August eighteenth, is really a great day," she added. "Sixty-eight years ago today, August eighteenth, 1920, the nineteenth amendment was passed, giving us, the women of America, the right to vote."

Then, turning back to her family, she said, "Twenty-nine years ago today, one of the happiest days of our life, our precious girl was born. We named her Dorothy after grandmother Bush, and Dorothy means gift from God and that she's certainly been. Now, this evening, my most beloved husband will accept the nomination for the presidency of the United States. What a day!"

Later in the day George and Barbara joined the Quayles at a hokey fund-raiser where all four rode in an antique truck toward a façade of the White House. But nothing could diminish Barbara's spirit, not even, she said, her fleeting thought as she dressed for the evening that Nancy Reagan had worn the same dress to the convention that she had worn eight years earlier. "I groaned," Barbara said. "I could never fit into the same dress from eight years ago."

She was clearly feeling fine when she gave her big speech Thursday night. It was .short, but filled with humor and affection, homey portraits and loving praise of her family:

"You're looking at a woman who couldn't be happier with her life," Barbara told her Republican audience. "That's a wonderful thing to be able to say. I have my causes, such as literacy. I have caring friends, such as yourselves. I have five wonderful children, each of whom has married an equally wonderful person, and in turn given me ten exquisite grandchildren.

"And I'm married to an absolutely marvelous man—and I want to take a few minutes to tell you why he should be president of the United States. I've loved George Bush since the day I laid eyes on him. Now I realize that won't get him a lot of votes. So let me explain why I respect him.

"First of all, George was always there when the children needed him. You've probably heard to the point you're sick of hearing it of all the important, big-deal jobs George has held. And he has. All those jobs have demanded tremendous energy and commitment from him. But do you know what

I respect about George? In spite of all those important, time-consuming jobs, our family has always felt an enormous part of his life.

"The children and I have always felt as important as the work he was doing. This has given our children confidence. . . . A reporter once asked George what his proudest accomplishment was. He said that the kids still come home. He meant it.

"He's just always there when someone needs him. I'm not going to tell you when this happened or where this happened or the events leading up to it, but my husband once had to fire a man who was an alcoholic. He didn't pass this painful task off to someone else; he did it himself. But George just didn't fire the man. First, as support, he went with him to tell his wife. She said, 'Thank God. For ten years I've worried and wondered why no one knew.' It was as if a burden had been lifted from her. And then do you know what George did? He attended AA meetings with the man. And today that man is a friend and supporter of my husband's. He may be in the audience tonight.

"George has always been there when I needed him, too. The hardest thing we ever faced together was the loss of a child. I was very strong over the months we were trying to save her. At least, I thought I was strong. Maybe I was just pretending. But when she was gone, I fell apart.

"But George wouldn't let me retreat into my grief. He made me share it and accept that his sorrow was as great as my own. He simply wouldn't allow my grief to divide us and push us apart, which is what happens so often when there is a loss like that.

"And for as long as I live, I will respect my husband for the strength of his understanding.

"I guess what I'm trying to say to each of you here tonight is that you should feel proud of what you have done at this convention. And what you have done is this—you've nominated for the presidency a man who is as strong and caring and decent as America herself."

The Bushes left the convention in an upbeat mood, flying to Indiana to showcase George's vice presidential choice, Dan Quayle. Barbara, upset by the early negative reaction to the senator, did what she could do help create a warmer atmosphere. The Bushes invited the Quayle family to a barbecue in early September. Barbara, no doubt recalling her own earlier days, was struck by the heavy demands on Marilyn Quayle, the only wife among the presidential and vice presidential candidates who still had young children—ages fourteen, eleven, and nine. "She still has to worry about dentists and homework and piano lessons," Barbara said. "What a juggling act."

From Labor Day until the November 8 election, the candidates, their wives, and families were on the road campaigning almost nonstop, and all of them had some testy moments. One of Barbara's occurred in Roanoke, Virginia, where a reporter asked how George Bush could enjoy his sleek speedboat, *Fidelity,* when people were starving in America.

Barbara smiled, not warmly, then replied, "The American people love boats. Everybody has to relax—and I've got sunblock on but that light of yours is much too close to my face and it's burning me."

But there also were lighter moments. Barbara was campaigning with country music star Loretta Lynn and noticed that the singer was a gum chewer. "Can you sing with chewing gum?" she asked. Loretta Lynn said that she could indeed, at least while she was in "Lake Tahoe or in a real dry climate." But elsewhere, she said, "I just put it on my back tooth and let it lay there."

Barbara spent more than half her time on the road with George. Both of them preferred it that way and figured it was a luxury they could afford in this campaign, so unlike the days when they faced the problem of "George Who?"

When Barbara traveled alone, many of her appearances were at women's clubs, hospitals, programs for the elderly, day-care centers, and elementary schools. She asked her schedulers not to send her to high schools and colleges, fearing a generation gap.

"I'm not just one who can stand to jolly up the crowd, you know, sort of cheer along," she said. "I think they need younger people and we've got all these sons. I don't see myself as a great campaigner."

But, she added, "I love people so I'm very good, I think, at hospitals. I don't think I'm so bad at elementary schools . . . I feel very strongly about my literacy program, programs for abused children."[4]

Barbara was direct with older children, broaching worldly subjects likely to interest them. Visiting a group of sixth graders at a Catholic school in Philadelphia in early September, she recounted how she had met Pope John Paul.

"One of my children [Marvin] was ill at the time and one of my grandchildren asked the pope to pray for him," Barbara said. "He did and he became better. Someday I hope you'll be lucky enough to meet his holiness, the pope."

She also had an easy time with younger children, being one of the few people on the campaign trail who looked comfortable in a classroom and avoided the effusiveness that adults often display on such occasions.

In Fayetteville, Arkansas, she visited four- and-five-year-olds at a Baptist day-care center. She walked in with a present for the children, a book titled *Blueberries for Sal*.

Holding up the book, she said, "I pick blueberries in Maine. Maine is one of the four hometown states for my husband."

The children in turn had a gift for her, a homemade basket filled with apples straight from the tree. Barbara accepted graciously, but not with false enthusiasm. "Pretty nice," she said.

At a school for disturbed children in Tulsa, Oklahoma, she read a story to a group of ten-year-old boys. As she was leaving, one came up and asked for a hug.

"As I leaned down, I heard someone else say, 'Don't forget me,' " Barbara reported. "The next thing I knew, I had an armload of all those precious children hugging and kissing. I could hardly keep from weeping, and I heard an emotion-filled voice behind me say, 'We wouldn't need all those expensive programs if these little ones were given love in the first place.' It was one of my Secret Service agents."[5]

Barbara's easy manner in small crowds led not only children but also grown women to approach her as if she were a favorite neighbor.

"Barb, I love your hair," a fifty-seven-year-old salt-and-pepper-haired volunteer told her at a children's hospital in Tulsa. Barbara laughed, not taking offense at this familiar form of address from a stranger. Then, looking at the woman's hair, she replied, "You're not there."

In Enid, Oklahoma, a woman said, "Those pearls must be awful special. I see you with them all the time." Barbara, who later would reveal that she wore the pearls to cover up her wrinkled neck, said with a smile, "They're all different and they're all fake."[6]

The big event in September was a televised debate between George Bush and Michael Dukakis. Barbara watched it with two of her children's spouses—Billy LeBlond, husband of Doro, and Margaret Bush, wife of Marvin. Afterward, according to campaign officials, she gave her husband some advice, which he took. She thought that his response to a question on the homeless had been inadequate and that his attacks on Dukakis were too strong.

By October, a month before the election, many Americans could identify Barbara by sight. Kitty Dukakis had not fared as well, according to polls taken at the time. Ironically enough, Barbara's white hair was the key difference.

John Molloy, author of a book titled *Dress for Success,* told United Press International that neither Mrs. Bush nor Mrs. Dukakis had made an especially strong impression, but Barbara's hair had stuck in people's memories.

"The first thing they said about Bush's wife is she looks very old, probably the gray hair," Molloy said, citing a survey. Most people, especially men, "didn't know what Mrs.

Dukakis looked like," he added. "She didn't make an impression, good or bad."

The survey also found that most people did not want Barbara Bush to change her hair and men felt most strongly on the point. "The men said, 'Oh no, she's that way. It's sort of like going back on what you are.' "

Barbara, always organized, managed to look neat and fresh on the campaign trail most of the time, despite days that might include ten different stops and a plane ride in between. She kept a bag of toiletries packed at all times and tried to coordinate the clothes she took on her trips—usually choosing skirts and dresses in blue, black, or brown—so she wouldn't have to take so many shoes.

One day a reporter complimented her suit, a brown skirt and light blue jacket. "It's Bill Blass," Barbara said. "Describe it as more practical than beautiful, but pretty stylish. The jacket can be worn separately. I think I've worn it every other day on the campaign."[7]

Barbara's style and common sense reminded some people of Eleanor Roosevelt, but she rejected that idea with some vehemence, saying there were other First Ladies who would make better role models.

"The ones I respected the most are the ones who did their own thing," Barbara said. "I wish you wouldn't say Eleanor. I grew up in a household that really detested her. She just irritated my mother.

"I admire Pat Nixon for some reasons, Betty Ford for some reasons. Mrs. Nixon was one of the most courageous, loyal women I've ever known. She was the most down to earth. A lovely lady. And Betty Ford, almost now more than then, I admire her enormously. She's in great pain. She goes around the country working for arthritis, working for drug abuse programs."

She might have added that all of them were lucky in another respect—they no longer had to campaign.

By mid-October Barbara confessed that she was "counting every single second" until election day. "I'm ready for it to end now," she said.

Much to her dismay, she had gained thirteen pounds during the campaign. She complained she was "the only living human" who gained weight under such circumstances—her daughter Doro had actually lost fifteen pounds.

"I am the world's most disciplined soul except for one thing—food," she said. "I write all my letters, I keep my diary, pay my bills, fix the scrapbook, I'm just very disciplined. But I just fall apart when it comes to food."

She said there was no particular food that tempted her—it was just the idea of eating. "Just anything," she said. "That's how I deal with tension. I just go eat something. It's like, 'That'll show that person who said that ugly thing.' "

She said that when she and George were alone, they ate simply, but "I think we're every doctor's horror. Last week we had an evening home alone and we had cheese omelets, bacon, and toast. Just the wrong things of course."[8]

True to her word, however, she was tightly disciplined about everything else. She carried needlepoint and a book on the campaign trail so she would have something to do during lulls and waiting periods. One handy addition to her purse was a pocket computer diary that held her schedule, her credit card numbers, a list of the books she had read over the past eight months, the names and addresses of 154 friends, the sizes of her children's clothes, and a reminder of two baby presents that were overdue. She also carried a plastic-covered three-ring binder that she used to record names, addresses, and ideas she picked up during the campaign.

Barbara successfully avoided controversy during most of the campaign. She complained about the widespread criticism of Dan Quayle, but in a mild way—"to take a very nice, good young man and trash him is not very nice."

Campaigning in California, she confessed that she had rooted for the Los Angeles Dodgers against the New York Mets in the playoff game leading up to the World Series and also favored the Dodgers over the Oakland Athletics in the series itself. But she had second thoughts about taking a stand, even about a baseball game. "I'll get in trouble for my Dodger answer," she told an aide afterward.

She still refused to answer questions about major issues of the day, but she did discuss them on her own sometimes in a way that put her husband in a good light.

"There is no question that we are better off today than we were in 1980 [when Democrat Jimmy Carter was president]," she said. "The Chinese are turning westward. Russia is negotiating for the very first time in my lifetime. We are doing away with weapons. The Russians are going out of Afghanistan. There seems to be some sort of movement in the Middle East. Things look better—they're not great but they are considerably better. Inflation is going down, unemployment is down, interest rates are down. I think things are better today."

Then, she added with a smile, "having said that, I am no politician."

Barbara hated it when George was criticized, but she found late in the campaign that she also disliked some of the tactics the GOP used against Michael Dukakis. She objected strongly when the Illinois Republican State Central Committee charged that Dukakis was weak on crime and said "All the murderers and rapists and drug pushers and child molesters in Massachusetts vote for Michael Dukakis."

A day after Dukakis denounced the campaign literature as "garbage," Barbara appeared on a CBS news show and said she agreed with his assessment. She said she had asked campaign chairman James Baker about it, telling him "Jim, I don't like that and I knew George wouldn't."

And she had sympathy for Dukakis when the *Washington Post* and ABC released a poll the day of the second presidential debate showing Dukakis running six points behind Bush. "I thought it put a lot of pressure on him," she said.

But when Barbara was in Los Angeles for the debate, she was angered to see signs featuring George Bush's face with the words "It can't happen . . ." and then "here" written on his forehead.

Said Barbara, "My gut reaction was to stop and pull them all down. That's wonderfully cute and sort of a Mickey Mouse kind of politics."

Then, on a personal note, she added, "The most beautiful creature in the world and they've got the ugliest picture up."

During the final week of the campaign, Barbara spent a day on a chartered bus for a trip across Illinois. She was joined by country singers Crystal Gale, Peggy Sue, Moe Brandy, and Lee Greenwood. One of her stops was a school for the deaf in Jacksonville, Illinois, where she put in a plug for sign language.

"I've decided that I want to learn sign language," she said, "even though I seem to be all thumbs. It was an extraordinary visit, much like the one I had at the School for the Deaf in Fremont, Calif., except I was very impressed in Illinois with a class that taught siblings how to sign. In one particular class, there was a father, brothers, sisters, three cousins and even one little boy who wanted to learn how to sign so he could communicate with his friend. I remember I was surprised in Fremont to learn that some of the parents couldn't sign."[9]

With just days to go until the election, Barbara said both she and George were having trouble sleeping even though polls showed that he was running well ahead of Michael Dukakis.

Ever cautious, Barbara said she didn't "think the thing's in the bag," and she recalled her own first vote—it was for Thomas E. Dewey, the 1948 Republican presidential candidate who was thought to be a sure winner but lost in the end to Harry Truman.

Barbara said that she and George had talked about the possibility of losing, and he favored getting in a car and driving right out of Washington after the inauguration if that happened. She joked that she had objected, since as vice president he had always had the services of a chauffeur.

"I said, 'You'll leave by yourself because I'm not leaving the White House in a car with a man who's never driven in eight years.' "

She told reporters that her worst experience in the campaign occurred at a fund-raiser where the guest speaker was a comedian who told tasteless jokes about childbirth. The audience wasn't laughing and as she considered the whole scene, she said, she "got the giggles. The thing I hate is that fifteen hundred people think I thought that man was funny."

Another embarrassing moment, she said, was when she turned around at one event to thank the person who had introduced her and realized she didn't know who he was.

Her strangest gift was a live baby pig—not the easiest thing to accommodate on the campaign plane.

On election day, November 8, the Bushes went home to Houston along with their children and older grandchildren. They voted early—7:40 in the morning—by paper ballot at a Ramada Inn near the hotel where they live when in Texas. The sixty voters waiting in line let the candidate and his wife go first. Afterward they visited campaign headquarters, where banks of volunteers were calling supporters to make sure they voted. Bush called a few himself, noting that some of those manning the phones were the same people who had been there twenty-five years earlier when he first ran for office. "Very inspirational," he said. Then he went jogging and had lunch with an old friend.

That night supporters gathered at the Brown Convention Center to await the results. It wasn't long before the good news started to come in. Michael Dukakis telephoned Bush with congratulations after the California polls closed at eleven o'clock eastern time. Other calls soon followed—President Reagan, Democratic vice presidential candidate Lloyd Bentsen, Jesse Jackson, Dan Quayle, and Canadian Prime Minister Brian Mulroney. Nancy Reagan telephoned Barbara.

The two and a half months between the November election and the January 20 inauguration sped by, just as busy as the campaign had been. Barbara found herself deluged with requests for interviews and appearances. She took it in good spirits, although she said she felt she was "on the couch" most of the time, being asked how she felt about everything.

Once she was home again, though, she was able to achieve one of her immediate goals—she sent the family springer spaniel Millie to Kentucky to be bred, so that there would be puppies in the White House.

She and George spent Thanksgiving at Kennebunkport alone—all their children, tired from the campaign, were home or with other relatives. Barbara and longtime house-keeper Paola Rendon cooked the turkey and George carved it. They had blueberry pie for dessert.

At Christmas the Bushes sent out 90,000 cards to friends and campaign supporters, though they didn't sign each one individually. Barbara, for the eighth year in a row, put the crowning ornament on the national Christmas tree, and said she didn't want to relinquish the job to Marilyn Quayle, even though the task has traditionally been performed by the vice president's wife. "I would be offended if someone else did it," she said. "It's the only thing I've done more than anyone else."

In January Barbara had lunch in New York with Nancy Reagan and Raisa Gorbachev. When photographers asked the women to smile, Mrs. Gorbachev said, "We can't see you. That's why we don't smile." Barbara interjected, "How do you say cheese in Russian?" As the translator interpreted for Mrs. Gorbachev, everyone broke into smiles and laughter. This time, Nancy Reagan could hardly object to Barbara sharing center stage.

During inauguration week, hundreds of Bush family members crowded into the Capitol, twenty-eight of them staying at the White House, including the grandchildren. Barbara, accustomed to the hullaballoo, was delighted to have them. "We get enormous strength from our family," she said. "It's always been like that and more so now. Once you're in a position where you're really isolated from people, you count more heavily on your children and your closest friends."

She said she and George would continue to go to local restaurants and theaters and make other short trips that put them in touch with normal life because "It's very good for both of us to get out of the house, be among people who come up and talk to you."

On inauguration day, Barbara wore a turquoise wool coat for the official ceremony. She stood by George's side as he was sworn in, a slight smile in evidence as he took the oath of office. George said later that she had saved him from embarrassment—after he was sworn in, he and Ronald Reagan left the inaugural platform and walked to the front of the Capitol to say a formal farewell. As the Reagans' helicopter left, the House sergeant-of-arms came forward to direct Bush.

"Mr. President," he said.

Bush didn't respond.

"I'm standing there, waiting for President Reagan," Bush told congressional leaders later that day, "and I feel something that was between an affectionate hug and kidney punch—the Silver Fox [his name for Barbara] telling me to get going."

Bush was inaugurated on a bright, sunny day, and he and Barbara got out of their limousine during the inaugural parade to walk. They held hands along the way.

When they reached the reviewing stand, Bush found a blond grandchild standing in his chair. He whisked her to the floor with a twirl, but his attention was soon diverted by a grandson showing him a Transformer. And so it went for the rest of the afternoon—wave to the crowd, talk to the children.

The evening, however, was reserved for grown-ups.

The Bushes had arranged inaugural balls at nine sites around the city to accommodate the thousands of people who wanted to attend, and they danced at each one, beginning at Union Station.

"You can say you saw here first a lousy dancer trying to dance the first dance with the First Lady of the United States," Bush said. Then, to the strains of "I Could Have Danced All Night," he took Barbara out on the floor. She wore a bright blue dress with a velvet top and satin skirt, designed by Arnold Scaasi. She said that blue was George's favorite color.

The Bush dance at each ball was short, but then, George had told Barbara four decades earlier that he wasn't much of a dancer. And anyway, they needed to get home. They had a big day—four years' worth of big days, in fact—ahead of them.

Moving In

A couple of weeks before Barbara Bush moved into the White House, Nancy Reagan took her on a tour of the family quarters, including the second-floor kitchen and third-floor laundry, which she hadn't seen before.

Afterward Barbara was full of enthusiasm. "It's the most beautiful house I have ever seen," she said. "I'm not going to change one thing."

As it turned out, she did make quite a few changes—among them making room among Nancy Reagan's bank of hair dryers for First Dog Millie's new puppies.

But perhaps the biggest change was in the atmosphere at the White House. George and Barbara Bush were both excited at the historic surroundings, and they invited scores of people in to share the fun of their discoveries. The quiet, formal world of the Reagans gave way to the more boisterous and open life-style of the Bushes.

Their first day in the White House was a Saturday, and they celebrated with a personal welcome to four hundred tourists waiting outside the gates. George Bush randomly selected fifteen people from the group and took them through the rooms himself. "This is the people's house and it does seem appropriate on this first day that we welcome as many as we can," he said.

The Bushes brought to the White House their own bed and all their bedroom furniture as well as pieces from their sitting room and living room. Barbara also packed a roomful of toys she had kept at the vice presidential mansion for her grandchildren, but other items were sent to the Bush summer house in Kennebunkport or to Camp David, the presidential retreat in Maryland.

During their first weeks in the White House, the Bushes settled into a routine. Each tended to business during the day—charity work, meetings, and interviews for Barbara, briefings, public appearances, planning sessions for the president—and they returned to the family quarters about six o'clock. The evenings were devoted to more work but also entertainment—family, friends, and staff, lots of them. They were seldom alone.

"We just like to have people around," Barbara said. "That's neither bad nor good. That's us."

Most of those invited to the White House got a full tour from Barbara. "Everything glistens," she said, showing the house off to reporters in early February. "It's so much more beautiful than I thought. Everything is beautiful in the White House. Honestly. The food is the most beautiful food you've ever laid your eyes on. Today I had lunch off of Wilson's plates, sometimes I have lunch off of Lincoln's plates, or Grover Cleveland's."

Moving to a window in the Yellow Room that showed off the South Lawn of the White House as well as the Washington Monument and Jefferson Memorial, she said, "This is the view right here. It's sensational." She remembered the room being yellow when Lyndon Johnson was president—he had invited the Bushes to the White House when George was first elected to Congress from Texas.

The White House bedrooms also drew rave reviews. Barbara noted that England's Queen Mother had slept in the Queen's Bedroom, along with a number of other real queens. She pointed out a secret stairway to the third floor, showed off the room where her grandchildren slept, and took a practical view of the historic Lincoln Bedroom. "It's not a thing of great beauty," she said, "but pretty exciting" with the only signed and dated copy of the Gettysburg Address displayed in one corner.

Barbara said she had become comfortable in the White House quickly and in the first weeks of the new administration was enjoying it much more than she had anticipated. "It's much more fun than I thought it would be," she said, adding that she would strive to keep herself from becoming isolated in all the splendor.

"I'm working on a theory," she said. "I'm going to go out so much that you're going to be saying 'Ho hum, there's Mrs. Bush out again.' I'm going to go to museums, I'm going to walk. I'm going to go out with friends. I'm just going to do things because I think there's a danger in . . . I mean look how pretty it is, who'd ever want to leave it. But I think it's very important to get out."

Because she had become accustomed to nonstop attention during the presidential campaign, she was prepared for the spotlight, but she admitted she still found it disconcerting at times.

"We grew up in a world where you didn't talk about yourself all the time," she said. "I will confess, this whole fall I felt like I'd been on the couch. I still look in the mirror and see a young sixteen-year-old whose tennis game could improve. But that isn't the way it is really."

She was delighted to find that after years of being harangued about her white hair and full figure, she suddenly was getting widespread acceptance of her looks—and appeared to be gaining popularity for her personality to boot.

She couldn't say why, except that "I think people know I'm fair and I like children and I love my husband. I think people like that. People think it's nice to think you really love your husband and your children and your dog—I don't even mind cats."

She said she had no plans to change her style—"I'm so old now that I don't have to pretend to be something I'm not"—

and she had nothing but positive things to say about her much-criticized predecessor.

"Of course I'm not going to be the same," she said. "She's a perfectionist and I'm not. Our life-styles are very, very different. Would I like to be like her? You bet. But there's no chance of that . . . she has a flair that I'll never have. But that doesn't worry me because I'm going to have something she didn't have. I don't know what it is yet, but we'll find it, whatever it is. I'm not going to worry about that. Remember I've got George Bush."[1]

Barbara made clear that she didn't plan to talk about the big issues of the day in public, but she was willing to comment on situations that interested her, usually involving women and work and literacy.

She noted that an abortion had been performed on a woman who had fallen into a coma after a car accident in a case that drew national attention. While groups opposed to abortion had protested the decision, Barbara said, "I agree with my husband on that. The life of the mother was at risk. I'm very grateful that it worked out as it did."

She still worried about mothers going to work when their children are young but said she realized it was an economic necessity for many. "There is a conflict there," she said. "But having said that, it's a fact of life."

While Barbara had been a full-time housewife ever since her children were born, she understood the budget pressures other families faced. She said that when she and George moved to Washington in the 1960s they had dipped into their oil earnings because they could not maintain a home in Washington and one in Houston and send their children to private schools on George's salary as a member of Congress.

"Could we have lived on it? We probably could have," she said, but it would have meant a major change in life-style.

Two weeks after she became First Lady, Barbara ventured briefly into a hot and emotional topic—gun control—and came to regret her comments.

Although George Bush was a member of the National

Rifle Association, Barbara told reporters, "I myself do not own a gun. I'm afraid of them. I'm too afraid I'd shoot the wrong person."

She described her first—and only—experience hunting with her husband.

"I went hunting with George once," she said. "He told me to follow the bird and I followed the bird and his head came right through that little circle [the rifle scope]. I put down the gun and said, 'That's it. I'm not going to do that again.' "

The discussion turned to a tragedy in California, where a gunman using a Chinese AK-47 assault rifle had killed five children in a schoolyard. Barbara said she thought such weapons were illegal and added: "They should be—absolutely."

To her chagrin, however, assault rifles were not illegal, and George Bush did not favor a ban on them. A few weeks later Mrs. Bush's press secretary, Anna Perez, announced that the First Lady would not be talking about gun control—or other controversial matters—anymore.

Barbara also found that almost everything she and her family did, no matter how insignificant, was of interest to the public, hungry for information about the new First Family. "I guess I'm going to have to start thinking more," she said.

But that wasn't really necessary with Millie around. She filled the Bush anecdote quota during the early weeks of the administration. Her puppies got a stupendous amount of attention; at one point, more than one hundred photographers were on the White House grounds taking their pictures.

George Bush revealed in the final days of Millie's pregnancy that he had been banished to the Lincoln Room because Millie didn't like her own bed and wanted to be with Barbara. "The dog refuses to go to the dog house," he said.

Both of the Bushes got teary-eyed watching Millie have her puppies. George said afterward it was "really beautiful. It was unbelievable." Asked if it was his first delivery, he said,

"Yes, first dog delivery." Barbara then put an arm around his waist and added that George had not seen any of his children born either.

She teased him about Millie too. Visiting an adult learning center in Baltimore where questions about the dog came up, Barbara revealed that Millie liked to take showers. "Millie, of course, doesn't take them alone because she's too short to reach up," Barbara said. "But someone, a very high public official, elected to office, takes a shower with Millie every week or so."

As she left the center, she had second thoughts about her revelation. "I hope that same public official won't be sore at me," she said.

With the obvious affection she had for Millie, Barbara shocked some television viewers a few months later when she kicked the dog while the cameras were rolling. The incident occurred while ABC was filming a "Prime Time Live" show featuring a tour through the White House conducted by George and Barbara, with Millie tagging along. Millie, having no sense of decorum, lay down in the Green Room during the taping and began to lick her private parts. Barbara gave the dog a kick to get her to stop and ABC correspondent Sam Donaldson also chastized Millie. Asked about the incident later, Barbara grinned. "I was just trying to get Millie to clean up her act," she said.

One setback the Bushes suffered early on in the White House was illness—George, Barbara, and Millie all developed Graves disease, a hyperthyroid condition that in Barbara caused an eighteen-pound weight loss in two weeks and vision problems that left her with puffy eyes.

After she disclosed the illness publicly, she was besieged with questions and concerns for her welfare, all of which she found somewhat irritating. In March she told a group of volunteers that, yes, she was feeling pretty tired—but then went on to recite what kind of a day she had put in: "I got up at eight and played tennis with three friends. I worked at my desk for two hours. I went to a lunch with George Bush. I just met with Martha Graham upstairs. I'm meeting with you now. And George and I are having a large reception this evening. Thank you for asking how I feel. I feel wonderfully well."

In April she was treated with a radioactive iodine solution to shrink her thyroid gland, but she continued to have vision problems, including periods of double vision. In November she went to the famed Mayo Clinic to see if doctors there could eliminate the eye problems. They changed her medication, and two months later she started radiation therapy at Walter Reed Army Medical Center in suburban Washington.

The treatments, given over a ten-day period, helped somewhat, but when they were completed, Barbara said she still had double vision at times even though she felt her eyes looked better. She said she and her husband had worried how the treatments would affect her personality, since there had been "an enormous change" in their daughter Robin during her radiation treatments for leukemia.

"So far everybody says I've been just angelic," Barbara joked. "I haven't changed a bit. I'm just as mean as ever."

Although the eye problems never did disappear entirely, they didn't slow Barbara down much. After her first one hundred days in the White House, she found that she was not as isolated as she had feared. She went out frequently to charity events, museums, visits to friends, restaurants, just as she had said she would. She and the president read six newspapers each morning while watching the early television news shows on three channels. In the evening, they watched four news shows.

"The world comes to you," she said. "I mean, we're not as isolated as you might think. We've seen thousands of people." And those who couldn't manage to see her often wrote instead. In her first three months in the White House, she received 35,000 letters.

She often went to the "back fence" to talk with tourists and sometimes watched them from a White House window, noting with amusement that Americans who took a picture of the White House frequently started on the sidewalk, then backed into the street to get everything in, whereas Japanese simply crossed the street and took the picture from Lafayette Park.

She still managed to exercise, usually seventy-two laps daily in the pool on the White House grounds—under the watchful eye of a Secret Service agent. "Someone watches me swim a mile every day," she said. "Talk about watching grass grow."

To relax, she said, she and George watched movies and some television shows, including *Murder, She Wrote* and *Sixty Minutes*, often with friends. She read short mysteries in the evenings, but with her full days and 6:00 A.M. rising time she had trouble staying awake.

"By nine-thirty I am ready to go to bed," she said. "So I go to bed to read a book. I barely can keep my eyes open. He wanders in about ten."

She thought her fatigue might have been caused by her thyroid condition. "I'm lucky if I get through the day," she said. "I don't mean I'm overextended, but I am sixty-three years old and I need to be babied a bit."

She decided on her own schedule and thought perhaps she was trying to do too much. "Nobody asks me to do all these things," she said. "I do them because I want to. But I have over-scheduled myself. I'm not going to go into retirement. I'm just not going to try to do twelve events in one day. That's silly."[2]

Despite her age and her ailment, Barbara kept up the full social schedule that she and George had long maintained. It was not unusual for her to come home from a full day of events to a house full of guests. While she now had many helpers to take care of the cleaning, decorating, cooking, and cleanup, she nevertheless had to be on hand to help entertain.

Frequently guests were invited to a buffet with a movie afterward—usually the first runs of the day—*Working Girl, Beaches, New York Stories, Major League, Chances Are.*

Or guests would pile into cars and go to the president's

favorite Chinese restaurant in the nearby Virginia suburbs. By spring Bush had opened a horseshoe pit, and he celebrated by holding a party around it—hamburgers, hot dogs, and a competitive game.

The guests included members of Congress, old friends, reporters, Cabinet members, governors, business leaders, sports stars and team owners, authors, members of the Supreme Court, and members of the White House staff.

Because the open-house style of the Bushes contrasted sharply with the closed society of the eight Reagan years, many people were surprised at the ongoing festivities at the White House. But those who had known the Bushes earlier recognized this party fever as just a continuation of their longtime penchant for entertaining.

"So what's new?" Barbara said. "That's the way it's been for forty-four years."

She recalled that during their time in New York City, living at the Waldorf-Astoria while George was ambassador to the United Nations, he called home one night and said: " 'I've just been to a wonderful meeting and I asked all the newspaper publishers and their wives to come back for a drink.' I mean, we didn't have a kitchen there but we also had a hotel so we could cope," Barbara said. She added that she didn't mind such impromptu invitations. "With George nothing's impossible. What's more, he's willing to help, not dump it all off on me."[3]

For the formal White House dinners, the Bushes worked on the seating plans themselves. When the social office drew up a plan and sent it to them, the arrangements would often come back with revisions.

The same planning went into the entertainment at Camp David and Kennebunkport, but arrangements at both those places were much looser. Going into her first summer in the White House, Barbara explained to *House and Garden* magazine how the family lived at Kennebunkport in August.

"The difference between Washington and Maine is night

and day," she said. "I play tennis, garden, and plot and plan everyone's day. I try to see that one and all are included in some activity. I do have certain rules posted on the doors, which no one really keeps:

PICNICS SHOULD BE PLANNED EARLY FOR THE BEACH. PLEASE PICK UP WET TOWELS AND USE THEM TWICE. PLEASE BE DOWN FOR BREAKFAST BETWEEN SEVEN AND NINE OR NO BREAKFAST.

"All rules are broken constantly."

She said the entire family—all the children and grandchildren, twenty-three in all—tried to be together in Maine at least for a few days in August.

"The decor of the house is hodgepodge," she said, "three houses of furniture put in one, no antiques, fifteen-year-old slipcovers—a house where grandchildren are more than welcome in. There are six bedrooms and six baths in the main house plus a girls' dormitory. My favorite room is the end room, painted aqua as it was in George's grandmother's time, with a large fireplace, latticework on the walls, and water on three sides."

She said her garden was in the same spot the old garden had been, a mix of perennials and annuals. "There is a cutting garden so I can have flowers for the house," she said. "I mix my garden flowers with wonderful wildflowers and have big loose arrangements. My favorites are hard to say, but certainly lilies, gardenias, daisies of all varieties, phlox, and delphiniums."

Her early-morning routine at Kennebunkport was similar to the one at the White House, but without all the newspapers.

"The day starts with coffee in bed at six—children and grandchildren drift on down. They all have breakfast at the dining-room table and there's a choice of pancakes or muffins, depending on the day. Many of us go our separate ways—boating, swimming, softball, tennis, horseshoes, and golf. Many ages play together.

"Lunch, usually on the deck, is a big pot of soup—clam chowder, corn chowder, zucchini—with sandwiches or salad. The children eat dinner early but the two older grandchildren usually eat with us. I do not cook these days. Most of our meals are cooked on the grill, swordfish being my favorite and lobster a close second. We usually have a clear soup served in mugs in the living room. A favorite dessert is ice cream with Paola Rendon's butterscotch sauce—she's been with us for years. We entertain a lot on four round tables of ten—big family dinners and get-togethers mixing childhood friends with foreign friends or just out-of-town guests."[4]

Among the foreign friends invited to Kennebunkport early in the administration were French President François Mitterrand and his wife Danielle. Although Mitterrand is a rather formal man by nature, he got into the spirit of the place, bringing along a plaid shirt, corduroys, and hiking boots but declining a ride in the president's high-speed boat *Fidelity* on grounds he gets seasick.

Later that year when the Bushes went to Kennebunkport for their traditional August vacation, the guests included Danish Prime Minister Poul Schlüter and his wife Anne Marie, whom George and Barbara had met in 1982 during their travels to Europe. Schlüter, who enjoys tennis and bicycling, was treated to a ride in *Fidelity*. A week later, Canadian Prime Minister Brian Mulroney, a sports enthusiast like Bush, and his wife, Mila, arrived with their four children, ranging in age from three to fifteen. Good friends of the Bushes, they were invited back repeatedly.

While almost all guests at Kennebunkport spend the night, fewer do in Washington, but Barbara still managed to keep the bedrooms at the White House pretty full.

Among those who slept in the famous bedrooms during the first months of the Bush administration were Kentucky horse breeder Will Farish, whose dog was the father of Millie's pups; childhood friend FitzGerald Bemiss, who was at the Bushes' wedding; Pennzoil chairman Baine Kerr; and former neighbor Shirley Pettis Roberson.

Although Mrs. Roberson was familiar with powerful Washington, having served two terms in Congress herself, she said staying overnight at the White House in a historic bedroom—she and her husband, Ben, were in the Queen's Bedroom—is "a storybook experience. . . . Every place you turn there is a sense of your forebears. Bar makes you feel you must know everything about this wonderful house, and because she knows every piece and tells its story, the whole floor comes alive."

Barbara had turned the Queen's Bedroom into a guest-room extraordinaire. A white princess telephone next to the four-poster bed came with instructions for dialing out and for obtaining White House services. A basket of fresh fruit was set nearby. In the adjoining bathroom she put a hair dryer and assorted toiletries, and she could reel off the names of the famous people who have been guests in the room— Prime Minister Winston Churchill, the English Queen Mother, Queen Elizabeth II, Queen Fredericka of Greece, and Queen Juliana of the Netherlands. During the inaugural ceremonies, George Bush's mother, Dorothy, was the honored guest.

When Barbara took guests on tours of the house, she also pointed out the Lincoln Sitting Room where Richard Nixon prayed with Henry Kissinger two nights before resigning as president. Taking reporters on a tour of the house, she said, "This is the little sitting room that's only notable because supposedly, remember, when President Nixon and Kissinger went in—it had a fire in the fireplace and air-conditioning on in July."

She also showed off the Bushes' private sitting area, a small room in the back of the White House that was used by Ronald Reagan as a study. Barbara put her big needlepoint rug on the floor and hung the mounted kimonos that she had displayed on the walls of the vice presidential mansion. Bush family photographs are on display around the room, which includes a television with a remote control bearing the presidential seal.

She and George usually eat dinner in the President's Dining Room, whose walls are covered with Revolutionary War scenes. The room was turned into a dining room by the Kennedys; earlier presidential families had to go to the first floor to eat.

"This used to be Tad Lincoln's and, much later, Alice Roosevelt's bedroom," Barbara said. "Jackie Kennedy made this an upstairs dining room."

She said that when Alice Roosevelt had the room around 1901, "there were no West Wing offices and in the other end of the hall from this room, all the affairs of state were conducted. Six children running up and down the hall . . . and the business being carried on in the other end!"[5]

The Bushes completely redid the president's office. "This room was the Treaty Room and it was very dark," Barbara said. "Jackie Kennedy changed it from the Monroe Room to the Treaty Room, and before the Monroe Room it was the president's office."

On the wall, George Bush had hung a picture of President Lincoln talking with generals aboard a riverboat on the Mississippi. He said he drew inspiration from it, seeing the president and his men as peacekeepers.

Among the framed and autographed pictures on the president's desk was one of Mulroney, who had written, "George, believe me it only gets better."

Behind the desk was the president's electric typewriter—he uses it himself—and a word processor that he would take lessons on later after he announced a new education plan and said he was going to be a student himself.

"George loves this room," Barbara said. "These were Nixon's old curtains. We found them in storage."

Before Barbara Bush had been in the White House a year, her popularity had soared. An NBC–*Wall Street Journal* poll found that Americans preferred her to Nancy Reagan by a three-to-one margin; at the same time, George Bush topped Ronald Reagan two to one.

American women began to emulate Barbara. The three-strand fake pearls she bought for ninety-five dollars became a big seller. The National Needlework Association said her interest in sewing had brought new adherents to the craft. And designer Arnold Scaasi said, "Having Barbara as First Lady means that women who weren't buying a new dress because they were a little overweight are buying new dresses now. It means you don't have to try to look like your daughter any more."

"Not since the 1950s has there been a first lady who so perfectly fitted our traditional ideas of how a First Lady should be," said Barbara Kellerman, a professor who had studied presidential families for a 1981 book, *All the President's Kin*.

"Mrs. Bush is really a throwback—in the good, not the pejorative sense of the word—to a time when what a First Lady did, how she looked and the activities in which she engaged seemed very clear to all of us, when there was some consensus of what was appropriate."[6]

Even lobbying groups that were vehemently opposed to the president's positions on social issues often had a kind word for Barbara.

Kate Michelman, executive director of the National Abortion Rights Action League, said that although Barbara publicly supported her husband's opposition to abortion and refused to say what her personal view was, she set a good example for politicians pondering the issue.

"She's why politicians should trust women to make decisions for themselves," Michelman said. "She's thoughtful, caring, concerned, and compassionate, not only about children's lives and the quality of family, but about the role of women in the society and the world at large."

Barbara herself said she was a liberal on social issues, but added that she considered the Republican Party to be liberal on social issues as well.

"Now you may not look at it that way or you may not look at me that way, but I think of us both as caring enormously about people and looking—it's very hard, you know, easy when you're one civilian, but when you're the president of the United States you have to look at all the people."

The Bush family had a discussion about abortion around the dinner table in January 1990, after Bush had been in office one year. *Newsweek* magazine reported that all the men at the table had been against abortion and the women for it, but George W. told reporters the report was "totally inaccurate." He said he didn't know what meeting the article referred to "nor do all the males come down on the same side." George said that he, like the president, was opposed to abortion, but that not all of his brothers agreed.

At the end of the Bushes' first year in the White House, the United States invaded Panama and ousted strongman Manuel Noriega. Women were prominent in several of the skirmishes that occurred. Barbara was asked, in an interview with reporters at the White House, what she thought about women in combat.

She replied that while she thought women would have no problem handling the job mentally or emotionally, she had reservations about the physical side. "The average man is better at throwing a hand grenade," she said. "I myself am very athletic but I have never been able to throw a ball as far as a man."

She said she also worried that most women would not be strong enough "to carry a buddy to safety" if his life were endangered.

But she had a clear opinion on a noncontroversial aspect of the war: the capture of Noriega. "He cost thousands of lives," she said. "He's a bad man. Also, I'm glad he's here and will stand trial."

Turning to a scandal of the day, Barbara said she was as shocked as the rest of the nation to find out that a white Boston man had killed his pregnant wife and then convinced police that the couple had been attacked by a black man, a story that later unraveled.

"First of all it made me sick," Barbara said. "All of it, the whole thing. I have to say I can understand what turned out to be an overreaction to this crazy man's story because it's inconceivable that a man would kill his own wife and shoot himself so he would be incapacitated."

But such grim subjects aside, Barbara said that after a year in the White House she was still surprised at how much she liked it. Completely gone was the pity she had expressed several years earlier for Nancy Reagan having to live in a fish bowl.

"The wife of the president of the United States is probably the most spoiled woman in the world," she said. "You'd have to be awfully spoiled if you lived the life we live and wished for something else."

Early in her second year as First Lady, she donated her inaugural ball gown to the Smithsonian Institution, a long-standing White House tradition.

She invited both her hairdresser, Yves Graux, and her favorite designer, Arnold Scaasi, to the museum for the occasion. "I vividly remember visiting here as a child," she said. "I remember the awe and the excitement I felt in our very own history. Who could have ever guessed that fate and an extraordinary husband would actually make me part of that history. I am grateful beyond words."

Her dress, blue satin and velvet, went onto a mannequin in the First Lady collection, along with the pearls she had worn to the inaugural, a cape, and an evening bag.

Barbara continued to get thousands of letters from admirers and she let it be known that some of them got on her nerves, however well meaning the sender.

As Mother's Day neared, she asked people not to send her cards, letters, or other endearments and expressed some irritation that people treated her as if she were part of their family, even though she didn't even know them.

"Please don't write me," she said. "I have children of my own. I'm not your mother."

She made the same request in anticipation of her sixty-fifth birthday, coming up just a month after Mother's Day.

"People who don't love you—I mean they like you but they don't love you—send you flowers and things," she said. "And it's so sweet. But it should be a very private, personal thing. So I walk around like Scrooge in this house saying, 'Anyone who mentions it, I'll cut off your head.' "

Barbara said she received hundreds of cards on her birthday from complete strangers and with her social sense felt obligated to answer each one.

"I just want to celebrate it with my husband and children and maybe one friend," she said, "and I can't think of that one."

Ironically enough, however, George was not home on her birthday that year—he was in Chicago on a fund-raising trip for Republican congressional candidates. The president told his audience that he had telephoned his "birthday girl" and found that "she seems unexcited about her sixty-fifth birthday."

And although she said she wanted a private celebration, Barbara spent part of her birthday in a very public forum, reading a story to a dozen children on ABC-TV's *Good Morning America.*

The children listened quietly but later blurted out, "Happy birthday, Mrs. Bush." She seemed genuinely pleased. "Oh, how'd you know?" she said. "Who told you that secret? Thank you very, very much."

Besides the unwanted birthday cards, Barbara had discovered another unpleasant aspect of the White House—the constant public interest in and media scrutiny of the entire First Family had been hard on her children, especially Doro, who had recently separated from her husband. Barbara expressed sympathy for John Kennedy, Jr., who had failed the bar exam a second time and prompted a New York tabloid to write: "Hunk Flunks."

She spoke out strongly against the new practice of some homosexual activists of revealing that someone was gay even when that person did not want the fact publicly known.

Noting that two Bush family friends had died of AIDS, Barbara said, "I think one of our friends was out and one wasn't. I'm not one who believes in outing. I really don't like that at all." If asked, Barbara said, she would be willing to appear in a public service announcement to help children with the disease.

On the positive side, Barbara said, she loved the opportunity to be part of such happy occasions as the release of a hostage from Beirut. She recounted how thrilled she had been to be with the president when he greeted former hostage Robert Polhill, and said she was moved to tears when Polhill telephoned Frank Reed, a hostage who had been released just hours earlier.

Animals continued to play a part in Barbara's life. She had two early summer encounters with them, one a lot of fun and one quite alarming.

The fun occurred on a fishing trip she took with her husband to Pintlala, Alabama. They fished on a fifty-five-acre private lake owned by Ray Scott, founder of the Bass Anglers Sportsman Society of America, who quoted longtime fishing buddy George Bush saying that "Barbara is the only person I know of who can fish and read a book at the same time."

Scott reported that on this outing, Barbara had not been reading, but she did carry on a lively conversation with him and "Who do you think caught the biggest bass? Barbara. It weighed six pounds and twelve ounces."

He laughed. "Then she had the nerve to turn to George, who was hunched over his rod in his boat about forty feet away. She said sweetly, 'George, darling, would you like to have your photograph taken with my fish?' "

But Barbara portrayed George as the hero of a misadventure she had at the White House swimming pool. She was moving along in the water for her mile-a-day swim when she encountered a large rat.

"I swim with a mask so as it went by right in front of me—I mean, it was enormous," she said. "Fortunately George Bush was there and drowned the beast. It was horrible."

The White House, surrounded by parks and munching tourists, has long had a problem with rats and mice. Barbara said that after her close encounter, she asked the guards to check the pool every day before she got in to make sure nothing else had gotten in ahead of her.

Barbara had two major foreign affairs duties in the spring-summer months of 1990. The first was a summit visit in May by Soviet leader Mikhail Gorbachev and his wife Raisa.

The Bushes had first met the Gorbachevs in 1985 when the vice president was sent to represent the United States at the funeral of Konstantin Chernenko, Gorbachev's predecessor. Barbara and Raisa talked during that visit at a tea following the funeral, and they hit it off immediately after discovering they had a common interest in education.

The two women found in subsequent meetings that they liked one another, and the goodwill held through the 1990 summit. Barbara took Raisa with her to Wellesley College for the famed graduation speech and invited her to visit historic Williamsburg, Virginia. Mrs. Gorbachev declined the Williamsburg trip, however, saying she preferred the alternative that was offered—a relaxing day at Camp David.

Two months later leaders of the seven big industrial powers had a meeting in Texas and Barbara entertained the wives—Sachiyo Kaifu of Japan, Danielle Mitterrand of France, Mila Mulroney of Canada, and Livia Andreotti of Italy. Denis Thatcher, husband of Prime Minister Margaret Thatcher, went off on his own, and Hannelore Kohl, wife of German Prime Minister Helmut Kohl, did not make the trip with her husband.

No matter. Barbara gave her four guests a first-class tour of Texas. Although the summit leaders met in Houston, she took the spouses off to San Antonio for a visit that included the Alamo, the symbol of Texas independence.

"Nobody can come to Texas without seeing the Alamo, so this is very special," she said.

The mayor of San Antonio, Lila Cockrell, made all the women honorary mayors of the city, leading Barbara to joke that the number of women mayors in the state had grown tremendously.

The women also visited the Mission San Jose, established in 1720, and watched a variety show at a restored theater. They weren't alone—the audience included a lively group of nine hundred children from the city's summer program.

It was the kind of outing many of the foreigners probably had not been on before, as Barbara acknowledged. "I wanted to show off a different part of Texas," she said. "I wanted them to see a side of Texas that you might not see anywhere else . . . a wonderful, exciting, thrilling city."

By the end of 1990, Barbara was back where she had been ten years earlier—up in a lift, putting an ornament atop the national Christmas tree.

For this occasion, she invited Doro's two children—six-year-old Sam and four-year-old Ellie, who wore the new red coat her grandmother had given her as a birthday present. The classmates of Sam and Ellie were on hand as well, urging Sam to jump as he rose in the lift.

All in all, it was a jolly occasion but it ended on a somewhat somber note.

Asked what she wanted most for Christmas, Barbara replied, "We're all wishing for peace. We want our people home."

It was not to be, though. A few weeks later, the United States was at war with Iraq.

The Gulf War

When President Bush announced on January 15, 1991, that America was going to war against Iraq, Barbara watched her husband on television along with the rest of the nation.

She was in the sitting room in the private quarters of the White House, a comfortable place made cozier by Barbara's needlepoint rug, the one that had much of the family's history woven right into the fabric.

Her daughter Doro was beside her, along with a family friend, evangelist Billy Graham.

Although Barbara didn't say much, "there was an intensity of focus that seemed singular to me at the time," a White House source said. "There is usually a lot more joking around her, a lot more teasing. There was none of that. There was just none of the usual razzing."

Barbara, like most Americans, was disappointed that Iraqi leader Saddam Hussein had failed to back down under the ultimatum the United Nations had issued—withdraw your troops from Kuwait or face a multinational attack.

For months after Saddam's August 2, 1990, invasion of neighboring Kuwait, Barbara had remained optimistic that war could be avoided.

Despite the crisis atmosphere that settled heavily over Washington, the Bushes decided to take their usual three-week August vacation in Kennebunkport. It was a calculated decision. The president remembered how Iran had succeeded in making Jimmy Carter a virtual prisoner in the White House—bogged down with work and worry—a decade earlier while Americans were held hostage in Tehran. Bush was determined that Saddam Hussein would not gain that same kind of power over him. So he went on vacation and made a show of enjoying himself.

But he spent much of his time in meetings with top aides, most of them looking out of place on Bush's oceanside deck with their white dress shirts and stiff black shoes.

The telephone calls from Washington, some jangling in the middle of the night to inform the president of the latest developments, were out of public view.

"You know you're not away in this job no matter where you are," Barbara said. "George even talked to one head of state from aboard the boat."

Barbara herself spent the vacation as she usually does, focusing on her twelve grandchildren, all of whom paid a visit at some time during the month.

She got up at five-thirty each morning with the arrival of Millie and Millie's pup Ranger. "My eyes would open and I'd go out and push the automatic coffeepot down, feed the dogs, walk them," Barbara said. "Then we'd climb back in bed and read the papers and the grandchildren all came down. We have that hour where we're watching the news and the kids are listening to their grandfather."[1]

When the children asked about the Gulf crisis, Barbara said, "I reminded them that a perfectly peaceful country was sitting there and another country invaded it and we cannot have that."

Like many parents and grandparents in the winding-down days of summer, Barbara spent a lot of time handing out Popsicles and supervising the children at the beach. Unlike most parents, she had to keep the children away from the house for long periods because foreign heads of state were meeting with the president there. When Prince Saud of Saudi Arabia came for a visit, the children were beside themselves with excitement, imaginations fired by tales of the Arabian Knights.

"Who could imagine what a full-fledged Arab prince looked like," Barbara said. "But I kept the children at the beach all day long. I thought it was a genius job on my part keeping them entertained."

She took some of the older ones shopping for back-to-school clothes and made sure they did their summer reading—*Tom Sawyer* for thirteen-year-old Noelle, daughter of Jeb and Columba.

When she wasn't with the children, Barbara went antiquing with Betsy Heminway and did some reading of her own—*The Burden of Proof,* a thriller by Scott Turow; *Slim,* an autobiography by Slim Keith; and *Memories of Midnight* by Sidney Sheldon.

She also made a point of getting a lot of exercise, swimming a mile each morning, not in the frigid Atlantic Ocean but a warmer pool. After that it was a stationary bike for an hour and in the afternoon a toning session with a tape on the VCR. "I really built myself up, darn it, to be very strong," she said.

Still, it was not a typical summer. Both Bushes had daily reminders of the hundreds of thousands of young Americans settling into the hot sands of Saudi Arabia, their futures uncertain, their present uncomfortable. Barbara, typically, looked at it from a mother's viewpoint.

"I hate it because families are being broken up," she said. "I feel just like any other mother would. How do you think George feels—that's what kills me—because he really feels each one of those [young soldiers] are his."

Her worry extended to the hundreds of foreigners—including Americans—who had been trapped in Iraq after Saddam's troops invaded Kuwait. Now they were being held hostage in Baghdad, and some were taken by force to chem-

ical and nuclear facilities that Saddam figured were most
likely to be bombed if the West decided to challenge his
invasion. Saddam denied the foreigners were hostages; he
said they were simply "guests" of his regime for the time
being.

In early September Barbara made a personal appeal to the
Iraqi leader to free the hostages. In an interview with Knight-
Ridder newspapers, she said: "Let your guests go and then
let's talk about this."

Asked how she would feel if she had a son or daughter
serving in the Gulf, Barbara replied with two voices, one
as a mother, one as the president's wife: "I'd be sick with
worry . . . but I would also feel very proud. They are the
only thing that's keeping any kind of peace in the Middle
East."

Early the next month Bush and Soviet leader Mikhail Gorbachev held a summit meeting in Finland. Barbara was on
the trip as well. She answered with icy anger when a reporter
asked if the president had sent the wrong image with his
high-profile Maine vacation while American soldiers were
shipping out to the desert.

"My husband spent most of the time on the telephone,"
she replied. "He was not going to become a hostage in the
White House to that dreadful man."

In another interview, she sought to put the vacation in
perspective. "There is a certain stability about Maine and that
was a reason George was there," she said. "You know this is
not the United States against Saddam Hussein. I think occasionally we forget that. George stayed in Maine because it
sent the right message."

During November the Bushes traveled to Europe for an
economic summit with other industrial powers, stopping
first in Czechoslovakia for a day. But even there, the Gulf
crisis was much on their minds. Barbara, visiting with a
group of eleven-year-olds, read excerpts from her book
about Millie and told the children that the dog had the run of
the White House, regularly attending meetings of the Na-

tional Security Council. "So Millie knows more about the Persian Gulf and Czechoslovakia than I do," she said.

For Thanksgiving, the Bushes visited the troops in Saudi Arabia, including those in Dhahran, just eighty miles from the Iraqi-guarded borders of Kuwait.

Barbara wore a camouflage jacket, khaki pants, white jogging shoes—and pearl earrings. She spent a lot of time posing for pictures with individual soldiers, signing autographs, and answering questions about Millie. "It is clear to me that Millie is the most popular member of the family," she said.

With the troops, she joked and teased.

"I feel like I'm signing checkbooks," she told a marine.

"I don't know whose camera I'm looking at," she said to another.

"You look familiar to me," she teased a third as she put her arm around his waist for a picture. "Didn't we just do this a minute ago?"

She had one Thanksgiving dinner with an army tactical unit, another with marines and British Desert Rats. She and the soldiers talked about their dogs and their kids, and she took names and promised to call their families when she got home.

Before the visit, Barbara had been shown how to put on a gas mask in case of an Iraqi chemical attack, but neither she nor the president carried their masks around. There was no escaping the guns and tanks, however. They were everywhere. "I rarely hug guns," Barbara said, pulling back when she came up against one on the arm of a marine.

General Norman Schwarzkopf, commander of the Gulf troops, watched her move easily among the soldiers and pronounced the Bush visit "wonderful for the troops."

"These kids here are so proud to be here," he said. "Doesn't it make you want to cry? It makes me want to cry."

E-4 Kelly Fischer of El Paso, Texas, was among the soldiers who saw the First Lady up close. "I admire her very much," the soldier said. "In fact I wanted to see her more than I wanted to see the president. That's terrible to say."[2]

Afterward Barbara said the visit had been "pretty exciting . . . and pretty moving."

"I was amazed by how many cameras the troops had," she said. "They asked us to autograph everything—pictures of their babies, pictures of their dogs, their springer spaniels. They asked me to sign pictures of their wives, their hats, their coats, their Bibles."

Like the soldiers, the Bushes brought home many souvenirs from the visit. The president revealed that he got "a little patch" from the famed British Desert Rats.

"We were sort of tucking things in pockets," Barbara said. "It was all very moving. I have to confess every time a helicopter took off, I felt like crying. It just—it seemed so final."[3]

She said she had been touched by her visit to the *Nassau,* an amphibious assault ship stationed in Saudi Arabia, where one sailor who had a wife and four children at home passed her a note that said: "Don't forget our wives, who are so courageous at home. They're really the brave ones. You and the president keep them in your prayers."

Said Barbara, "I thought that was so sweet. We do pray every night."

She also started wearing a rough bracelet sold by a group for the benefit of the soldiers in the Gulf. Daughter Doro gave it to her, and she in turn bought bracelets for Marvin and his wife Margaret. "I wear it because I think it's very important for me to remember always," she said. "It snags your clothes and cuts into your arm at night, so you do remember."

Money from bracelet sales, she said, would provide "those wonderful voice messages that families can leave for their sons or daughters in Saudi Arabia. And it also facilitates telephone calls back home."[4]

On December 1, when the White House Christmas tree was delivered, Barbara was asked what her Christmas wish was.

"We wish for peace," she replied. "We want our people home."

Did she think there would be war?

"No," she said. "I have great faith."

A week into the new year, she visited schoolchildren at the Church of the Immaculate Conception in Washington and told them that "like everybody else in America," she and the president were praying for peace. "You may think the president is all-powerful, but he is not," she said. "He needs a lot of guidance from the Lord."

Around her neck, she wore a paper necklace made by kindergarteners. It was filled with doves.

But a week later, with Barbara watching from the White House sitting room, the president declared war on Iraq, and American bombers, along with other allied aircraft, began a steady, pounding attack on Saddam's forces.

Once the war began, the president's life became intensely busy and Barbara did what she could to make things easier for him. "I think she worked very hard to clear the decks for him, to provide a haven, a calm," a White House source said.

In normal times, a number of people ask Barbara to pass on messages or information to the president. Although she much prefers that anyone with something to say to George Bush talk to him instead of her, she usually complies with the requests.

"People would think of her as a back channel to the president, and on most occasions she would pass it on to the president," the White House source said. But during the war, "She started winnowing it. If she thought it wasn't something he needed to hear at that particular moment, she wouldn't pass it on. At this point during the war she was selective in what she passed on."

Barbara also became more selective about the White House guest list. The Bushes continued to entertain, but she made sure the guests were people he could have fun with, people who would not "hammer him about his conduct of the war, people he could relax with."

She was happy and amazed to find that her husband remembered little things about what was going on with the

Arriving in New Orleans for the Republican National Convention aboard the riverboat *Natchez* in 1988, the Bush family en masse. *Courtesy UPI/Bettmann Newsphotos.*

Vice President Bush, Barbara, their children, and ten grandchildren gather on Christmas Eve for a family portrait. *Courtesy UPI/Bettman Newsphotos.*

On the day before George's inauguration, Barbara enjoys the role of grandmother as she and her daughter-in-law, Sharon, entertain her grandchildren at Blair House. *Courtesy Bettmann.*

Barbara in 1990 at the opening of a new model program for babies handicapped by exposure to crack and/or the AIDS virus. *Courtesy Reuters/Bettmann.*

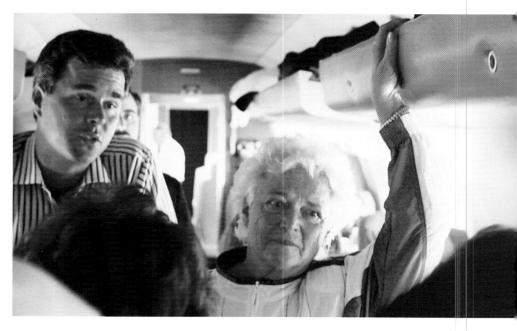

Barbara with her son Jeb en route to Costa Rica for the inauguration of President Rafael Calderón. *Courtesy Michael Kilian.*

Barbara with Costa Rican President Calderón and his wife, Gloria. The trip marked the first time Barbara had officially represented the United States at an important foreign ceremony. *Courtesy Michael Kilian.*

During George Bush's 1989 talks with British Prime Minister Margaret Thatcher, Barbara gives the Prime Minister's husband, Denis, a reciprocal kiss on the hand outside Number 10 Downing Street. *Courtesy Reuters/Bettmann.*

Watching over Millie and her six newborn pups in March of 1989.

As George Bush and Secretary of Defense Richard Cheney talk to the media about the Persian Gulf crisis in August of 1989, a worried Barbara looks on with Millie. *Courtesy UPI/Bettmann.*

An army trooper and Barbara share a smile and a turkey lunch on Thanksgiving Day, 1990, when George and his wife joined the troops in eastern Saudi Arabia. *Courtesy Bettmann.*

Following a presidential challenge to the troops during his Thanksgiving visit, a marine lance corporal chats with Barbara as they watch a Desert Storm vs. the President Horseshoe tournament at the White House in 1991. *Courtesy Reuters/ Bettman.*

children and grandchildren and asked about such events regularly despite his preoccupation with the war. But the children did their part to ease their father's burdens: "If the children were having problems in their own lives, they would not talk to their father about it," the White House source said. "When they called, it was very upbeat, stuff about the grandchildren."

Two days before the war started, Barbara had broken a bone in her leg while sledding at Camp David with her grandchildren, actor Arnold Schwarzenegger, and his wife, broadcaster Maria Shriver.

Although the president was standing at the top of the hill yelling "Bail out, bail out," Barbara held on to her saucer sled even after losing control of it. She crashed into a tree. The White House doctor looked at her injury and then sent her by ambulance to a hospital in nearby Hagerstown, Maryland. She returned to the White House later the same day, using a wheelchair from the helicopter on the South Lawn to the White House doors.

Although she didn't need a cast for the injury, Barbara was ordered to stay off her feet for a while, so during the first week of the war, she was mostly confined to the family quarters, using a wheelchair to get around.

Ten days after the accident, she made her first public appearance, hosting a reception for women taking part in a conference on breast cancer. She told reporters that her own experiences with her grandchildren made her realize how scared children are of the war and what parents can do to calm their fears.

She said a weekend at Camp David with Doro's children, Sam and Ellie, and Marvin's daughter, Marshall, illustrated for her that the youngsters were alarmed by the war footage on television. So she took time to sit down and discuss what was happening.

"We just talked about it, the things we were looking at," she said. "I answered their questions. They were little kids, so they didn't ask too many."

But she said they were especially alarmed when they saw the Scud missiles hit Tel Aviv. "They were saying 'Daddy, Daddy,'" Barbara said. She explained that what was happening was very far away from where they were, but that Americans were involved in the war, so it was still important to them.

"My kids aren't different than anyone else's," she said. "I just think parents should monitor their children and just be sure that they're understanding what they're seeing so they're not getting terrible nightmares. I just think you ought to be careful of your children."

Despite the children's fears, Barbara said, she agreed with the president on the need for war. "He did what he knew was right."

She described her husband as "steady and stable and calm. He's on the phone a lot of the time. He's like anybody else. Every single one of those soldiers are his."

At the end of January 1991, Barbara made her first out-of-town trip since the start of the war, flying to Boston for an event sponsored by the president's nephew, Jamie Bush. Fears of terrorist attacks were strong in Washington at the time, so security was extraordinarily tight for Barbara's visit.

The event was a benefit dinner at the Boston Park Plaza Hotel to honor students at the Mather School, who had been assured by a foundation of a fully paid college education if they graduated from high school. In the hotel, security men were stationed every twenty feet.

Barbara seemed absolutely at ease, even though she had to use a cane—a black wooden souvenir from Africa with her name on it—to get around. When a student asked what she thought of the war, she replied: "I don't like war but I am also thinking that one fella can't be allowed to brutalize a country. Sometimes it's easier to stay home and not do anything. This wasn't one of those times."

By mid-February, fear of terrorist attacks on airplanes had led to a dramatic fall-off of air traffic. Barbara, heeding the president's call to keep life as normal as possible during the war, decided to do her part. She took a commercial jet, a half full U.S. Air flight, from Washington to Indianapolis, flying coach.

"I am not afraid to fly," she said, adding that she and the president had discussed the problems besetting the airline industry. She said her trip "seemed like an important thing to do."

The airline industry was grateful: "We think it's a very positive move and will underscore the safe and secure nature of our system," a Pan American spokesman said.

Barbara was upset to find that some Americans were taking their anger at Iraq out on people in the United States who looked as if they might be of Arab extraction.

Telling reporters that tolerance would be her theme at commencement addresses in the spring, she described a sad letter she had received from a young girl in the Washington suburbs whose father, originally from Afghanistan, was a taxi driver.

"It was a wonderful letter saying she just didn't understand why—because people thought she was Arab that they came by and trashed her father's cab and hurt their house and scared them all to death. And she said, 'we're not Arabs, we're from Afghanistan.'

"Well, it didn't matter to me whether she—the story is a horrible story—it doesn't matter if she's Arab or not. What matters is, we don't turn on our fellow neighbors and citizens like that."

The incident led Barbara into thoughts about all kinds of tolerance, and how parents are the ones who instill such values in children. "I'm concerned about parenting correctly and tolerance," she said. "I'm concerned about sort of the sloppiness in not being tolerant of people who are different. Whether it's handicapped or racially different or religious differences or whatever, that concerns me a lot. And you know, I think the Desert Storm sort of made that all come into light because people worked side by side—I mean, Arabs and Jews and blacks and whites and Moslems and Christians and Catholics—their lives depended upon each other."

When those soldiers return home and find intolerance in their neighborhoods or on campus, she said, "It seems to me very sad."

Barbara followed the war day by day on television, along with everyone else, and she had her favorites among the Desert Storm military "briefers" who gave updates on the status of the war each day from both the Pentagon and the war headquarters in Riyadh, Saudi Arabia.

A reporter told Barbara that the president had mentioned her being in love with a different briefer every day.

"That's about true, too," she replied. "I did write Niall Irving [a British officer who briefed from Riyadh] a little note and got an adorable little note back from him. . . . I loved them all. They were all wonderful."

Toward the end of February, it was clear that the ground war, added to the six weeks of bombing Iraq had endured, was wearing down Baghdad's will. On February 27 Barbara visited six hundred marines and their families at a base in Quantico, Virginia, and told them the war was "very close to over."

"I think it's going to change the world," she said, adding that the world would be better because Saddam had been stopped.

The next day President Bush announced the end of the war. "Kuwait is liberated," he said. "The Iraqi army is defeated."

Like most Americans, Barbara was elated that the fighting had stopped. She was enthusiastic about going with the president to visit the nation's military bases in tribute to the men and women who had fought and to their families.

In early March she made a solo visit to the Mayport Naval Air Station in Jacksonville, Florida, and told the families they had been an important part of the war effort, simply by going about their daily lives while their spouses were at the front.

"Keep life at home on an even keel," she said. "This relieves their worries about you and it helps ensure a wonderful homecoming for them. By tending to daily life, by making sure that the dentist appointments are kept and the mortgage payments get made, the homework gets done, Little League games get watched, you are doing the most essential service of all."

Then she paused and told them she could empathize with what they had been through, from her own experience.

"You know, many years ago, when our country was fighting another just war, I was a college girl in Massachusetts. But my heart was not in the classroom. At least, that's how I explained my grades to my parents then. My heart and thoughts were somewhere in the Pacific on the USS *Jacinto*, a converted light cruiser, with a wonderful young naval pilot to whom I happened to be engaged. So we do understand a little bit of what you've been going through."

Life in the White House returned to normal, little by little. It had been closed to tourists during the war and for another month after, and Barbara said she was happy to have them back when it reopened in April. "I missed the tourists," she said. "I missed having them come through the house. And I felt—I think the house missed them too."

She said she was still getting letters related to the war, including an apology from a woman who had written her a testy letter earlier.

"She wrote and said, 'Please send my husband back—I don't think anything is worth his life and please tell your husband' . . . and I wrote her back and said, 'I can certainly understand how you feel and sometimes there are bigger things than we are and I'll pray for your husband.'

"So she evidently showed her husband her letter and my letter and he said to her, 'That's a very rude letter.' "

But Barbara said she hadn't considered the letter rude at all because she understood just how the woman felt. "I thought it was just exactly what a normal wife might write when she was desperate."

Like many people, Barbara was moved by the sight of an American soldier telling surrendering Iraqis who fell down and bowed at his feet, "Get up, get up, you're safe now." And she was amused to learn that many grateful Kuwaitis were naming their babies "Bush."

But she had nothing but loathing for Saddam Hussein, who remained in power despite the war, and she spoke out forcefully against him, causing something of a stir.

"I'd like to see him hung—if he were found guilty," she told reporters at a White House luncheon. "I mean, we're talking about thousands and thousands and thousands of lives that have been tortured and—I'm sure you have all talked to people who came back from Kuwait. But it's just horrible, the stories they tell."

She said she would not be opposed to putting him on trial for war crimes. "I guess he broke many, many international laws and I guess that would be only fair," she said. "He certainly is right up there with the people they tried during World War II."

Barbara's desire to see Saddam hanged was shared by so many Americans that her outspoken view caused the White House no political problems, but it did provide the president with some good opening lines in his speeches for several weeks. A few months later, when Barbara was once again venturing into controversial areas, someone reminded her that her marriage had survived the Saddam remark. She rolled her eyes and muttered: "Barely."

The war saw many young mothers unhappily going off to Saudi Arabia and leaving very young children behind with husbands or other relatives. The situation brought into conflict two of Barbara's strongly held beliefs—one, that women should be at home with their infant children, and two, that when you make a choice in life, you should strive to be happy with it instead of complaining. She resolved the conflict in this instance in favor of the mothers' doing their duty to country, saying she would not favor exempting military women with infants or young children from going to war.

"It's hard but you have to make choices in life," she said. "It's your choice. Nobody's making you do that. Now women who are in the service, particularly the reservists, will know what they've gotten into."

But the war also had reinforced one of her longest held and most cherished beliefs—that she had married a wonderful man.

"You know I would have told you that after forty-six years, you know your husband pretty well. But the truth is, I really was in awe of him. And I don't mean that I was going to fall down and kneel in front of him, but I just have enormous respect for his stability and his ability," she said. "I knew he had it, but these were very difficult times. And yet, he managed to stay on a very even keel with absolutely no blips. I think that's amazing."

Most of the nation seemed to share Barbara's opinion. The president's popularity soared in the weeks after the war ended. Bush himself reveled in the patriotic spirit that seemed to sweep over the country as a result of the quick victory in the Middle East.

The euphoria wouldn't last the year. But for several months, the mood of the country stayed high. For the Bushes, it was a satisfying end to a dark ordeal.

Travels with Barbara

Although Barbara grew up in an affluent, educated household, she never went abroad as a child or during her teen years. Once she married George, foreign travel was out of the question. There was a baby to raise, money was short in the early years, and the emphasis was on setting up a business that would support a growing family.

After George sold his oil holdings, there was plenty of money, but by then he was interested in building a political career and the Bushes spent their time shuttling between Texas and Washington.

So Barbara was quite excited when Gerald Ford chose George as America's envoy to China in the early 1970s when she was forty-six years old. It turned out to be one of the best experiences of her life, and she has been traveling around the world ever since.

During the eight years that George was vice president, Barbara frequently went with him on goodwill and diplomatic missions and to the many funerals of foreign dignitaries that American vice presidents are required to attend. In all, Barbara visited sixty-eight countries while she was Second Lady.

One of her most emotional trips was to Africa in 1985 to

call attention to areas struck by famine. During the weeklong visit, the emaciated children Barbara saw brought tears to her eyes.

"We're never going to be the same again," she said after walking through a refugee camp in the Sudan. Among the grisly sights were starving babies, their heads completely shaved except for one row of hair.

"They told us they had that so God can reach down and pull them up to heaven," she said.[1]

In the camp hospital, newborns had no incubators or sterile bottles. They were put on dirty cots among the sick. A nurse handed Barbara a four-pound premature infant—no rubber gloves, no surgical mask, no precautions.

"I couldn't help but compare, to think of our own premature grandchildren," she said. "We didn't touch them, you know. We put our hands in rubber gloves."

She also was struck by the size of the children. "When they told you the ages it made a tremendous difference in what you were seeing," she said. "What looked like a one-year-old was a four-year-old. If these kids live, they are going to be the strongest, most immune kids you've ever known."

Throughout the African tour, the Bushes were welcomed by crowds wherever they went because the people felt that such a high-ranking American official would bring more attention—and grain—to ease their sorrows.

Barbara recalled that she and the vice president were not always such welcome visitors. During an earlier visit to Afghanistan refugees in Pakistan, she said, women were crying and yelling at her. Despite the obvious anger in their faces, the interpreter told Barbara the women were saying "Thank you, Mrs. Bush, for the help you and your husband are bringing to us."

Annoyed at such a transparent lie, Barbara asked what the women were really saying. The interpreter obliged. What the women wanted was guns, not sympathy.

"Don't tell us you care," they said. "We don't give a darn

about that. Tell us you'll give us guns and we can go back and fight for our homes."[2]

Such goodwill trips were eye-openers for Barbara and helped her develop an appreciation for the severe problems in the wider world. But she also spent a lot of time in elegant diplomatic halls abroad and met the leaders who will be part of history, among them Anwar Sadat of Egypt, Rajiv Gandhi of India, Deng Xiaoping of China.

She tells a funny story about a dinner where she was seated next to Australian Prime Minister Malcolm Fraser.

"We were at a big formal dinner and I was too vain to wear my glasses," she says. "The first course was a big thing in the middle of the plate and I cracked right into it. The prime minister leaned over and whispered, 'Barbara, that's the adornment.' It was a lobster shell, which I naturally was trying to break and eat."[3]

That embarrassing gaffe sent Barbara to the eye doctor for a pair of contact lenses—with bifocals.

She had a better time when she first met Diana, wife of Prince Charles of England. Before Diana came to the United States, Barbara said, "I didn't think I'd like the little princess from England. But Diana is the most outgoing lady. I took her to a hospice. She sat on the beds of people who were in the last two weeks of life, held their hands and asked how they felt. They glowed. She said, 'How are you being helped? Is the program working? Are you in any pain? Does your medication help?' And these people told her."

At a dinner party during the visit, Diana was seated next to George Bush. Barbara said to her afterward, "I hope my husband behaved." Diana replied, "He didn't."

Then Barbara said, "She showed me that on his place card he had written: 'Stay awake. Only 29 and a half minutes and I guarantee you'll be asleep. That is, if the speeches and the music don't go on too long.' "

While the Reagans were in the White House, Barbara could travel anywhere and attract only minimal attention. But once

George became president, she found herself with a constant entourage. Reporters from the United States and the host country took great interest in every little thing she did.

Her first trip took place less than three weeks after she moved into the White House. She and George went to Canada. While George talked with Prime Minister Brian Mulroney about acid rain, Barbara went on a tour with Mila Mulroney, a friend from the vice presidential years.

One of their stops was a preschool—Mont St. Joseph Convent—in a suburb of Ottawa, where four-year-old Nicholas Mulroney was a student. The women read from a book titled *Owl Moon*. When the text called for hooting, Barbara gave it her all—"whoo, who, whooooooooooowhooooo"—to the delight of the Canadians, unaccustomed to such displays from first ladies.

Barbara also described her family to the children, telling them she had five children and eleven grandchildren, including one born that very week. She told them she spent three hours a day answering mail and that she worked for "the homeless, the hungry, people who have AIDS, and I work very, very hard for literacy. That's my big work, but it's all so much fun, so important, that I don't feel like it's work."

Afterward, a French-speaking correspondent said he had understood Barbara to say she was trying to make America "more liberal." An English-speaking colleague quickly corrected him: "more literate."

The Canadians were interested in Barbara's style, especially in comparison to Nancy Reagan's. The contrast could not have been more clear during the early 1989 visit. Instead of buying a new dress for the trip, Barbara wore the white Bill Blass dress she had chosen for the presidential swearing-in ceremony three weeks earlier, and with it an eight-year-old lavender coat.

Marci McDonald, Washington bureau chief for a popular Canadian magazine, *Maclean's,* said that after she wrote about Barbara's relaxed, natural style, "I got more requests for interviews about what this meant for Canadian women—could we stop holding our stomachs in and go a little easy on the wrinkle cream."[4]

The president described his meeting with the Canadian leader as upbeat. He said he had chosen Canada for his first trip outside the United States "to see that this strong relationship becomes even stronger."

He and Mulroney both pledged to try and reduce the damaging acid rain that fell on both countries.

Reporters also asked Barbara about acid rain since it was the centerpiece of her husband's visit, but she ignored the questions, making clear she did not want to get involved in policy issues.

Less than two weeks after the Canadian visit, the Bushes flew to Tokyo for the funeral of Emperor Hirohito. The emperor's death stirred anti-Japanese memories for some Americans since he had been a symbol of evil to the Allies during World War II. But Barbara urged the country to make an effort to look at Japan in a new light.

"George was shot down by the Japanese and if he doesn't feel embittered, I can't imagine why anybody else would," she said on the NBC *Today* show shortly before she left for Japan. "These are allies of ours and business partners of ours, and this is the time when you put aside old grudges and you move on."

Because the occasion was a funeral, Barbara kept a low profile in Tokyo. She had tea with Naoko Takeshita, wife of the Japanese prime minister, a dinner with other prominent women in the country, and another tea with Yolanda Salinas, wife of Mexican President Carlos Salinas—but no public appearances.

Among the Japanese women at the private dinner were two whom Barbara had known in Washington: Mitsuko Okawara, whose husband had been ambassador from 1980 to 1985 during the Bushes' vice presidential years, and Ise Togo, whose husband was ambassador from 1976 to 1980.

Barbara's style of travel differed markedly from Nancy

Reagan's, a distinction that was much noticed in Tokyo. While Nancy's entourage included a chief of staff, personal secretary, hairdresser, and personal maid, Barbara took along one personal assistant, Casey Healey, and her press secretary, Anna Perez. She also had refused to allow the White House advance team to make arrangements ahead of time, a fact that caused considerable confusion and grumbling among the press traveling with her.

After the funeral the Bushes made a brief stop in South Korea and then went on to China, where Barbara relaxed, acted like a tourist, and relived the days fourteen years earlier when she had been a resident of Beijing.

Right off she noticed that the city was undergoing a construction boom. Its physical appearance had changed substantially. "I mean, every place you look there's a crane," she said. "But the people are the same, the feeling is the same, the Forbidden City is the same."

She told reporters that her own experience in China "was about like now, except you weren't here. I used to ride my bike and give someone two cents to park it and spend an afternoon with a house guest."

When she tried to convey the emotions she was feeling about being back, the words came out in something of a jumble: "I feel good about China. I'm not good about telling my feelings. We went to church today. We saw the ministers we saw every Sunday when we lived here. This was a very happy time in our lives. I feel lucky to be able to be back here."

George Bush, speaking to the congregation at the church, also was feeling nostalgic. He said the church had been "our home away from home" when he and Barbara lived in China.

"It's a little different though," he said. "Today we came up with twenty motorcars in a motorcade and I used to come to church on my bicycle—my Flying Pigeon."

One of the pleasures of the trip was seeing old friends, people they had known in the early 1970s, both Chinese and foreign.

"We went to the International Club and saw our tennis-playing friends, the man who cut our hair," Barbara said. "We went to the U.S. Embassy. They brought back some folks who had worked in the embassy. We saw the widow of our driver and lots of good friends."

Among the highlights of the trip was a luncheon given for Mrs. Bush by the U.S. Embassy staff at an ancient ornate building known as Prince Gong's Mansion. In addition to the head table, there were eleven tables of three women each. Barbara moved among them, talking to everyone.

The women were all prominent Chinese—artists, teachers, authors, and doctors. Barbara gave a big hug to one of them, Huang Zhen, wife of a former Chinese ambassador to the United Nations, and she chatted happily with the others.

She was accompanied on her rounds by a Chinese woman dressed in a traditional long pink dress. When it was time to move to the next table—precisely four minutes was allotted to each one—the woman twirled and did a little dance.

Barbara's tour of the Forbidden City included a visit to the Hall of Supreme Harmony, a throne room that is off-limits to most tourists but was featured in the movie *The Last Emperor*.

The occasion was marred by Chinese security guards who roughly shoved reporters and photographers and slammed Barbara's own White House photographer, Carol Powers, into a doorway.

Barbara protested to the museum director, Yang Xin: "This girl's job is to take my picture and she got hit. Ask them to calm down."

Later Barbara told reporters that Miss Powers was fine, but White House Press Secretary Marlin Fitzwater had a different opinion.

"The Chinese security dislocated my fiancée's jaw," he said, revealing his engagement to Miss Powers for the first time.

During the visit, the Bushes gave a dinner for their Chinese hosts in the great Texas tradition—barbecued meat, baked beans, potato salad, and cold beer—all flown in from the United States especially for the occasion.

It was a big dinner for about five hundred people. Among the invited guests was China's leading dissident, physicist Fang Lizhi. Fang didn't make it to the dinner, however. Chinese officials stopped his car on the phony pretext of a traffic violation. Fang then tried to take a taxi, but it too was stopped.

The Bushes were unaware of what was happening during the banquet, but when they found out later, George told his hosts that he regretted Fang had not been allowed to attend. The Chinese authorities emphasized that they didn't want any American interference in China's "internal affairs," foreshadowing the stance they would take a few months later when the West protested the violent deaths of Chinese students demonstrating for democracy in Tiananmen Square. "We are heartbroken," Barbara said after watching the crackdown on TV with millions of other horrified people.

Three months after the China trip, Barbara and George took a weeklong trip to Europe for a meeting of NATO. While the European journey didn't have the sentimental value that China did, it was full of fun for Barbara, and without any underlying political tension.

On the plane to Europe, Barbara showed off a $7,000 gold watch from Tiffany's that she had received from the Ladies of the Senate, a club she had presided over for years. She said she was feeling good, except for her eyes, which were still red from her thyroid condition. "Now I forget what I look like," she said ruefully. "Maybe I look like this."

The first stop was Rome. Barbara, showing her practical side, wore a red suit with matching pumps for her initial event, but an hour later, when she was to tour the ruins of the Arch of Constantine, she switched from pumps to red loafers. Asked if she had changed into her walking shoes, she said, "You bet I did." Seeing the photographers' interest, she warned, "Now don't focus on my feet."

She also visited a center for homeless women, bringing

along a gift of six dozen sheets and towels. She helped serve food for almost half an hour and said afterward she was impressed with the facility.

That afternoon Barbara went for a swim at the U.S. Embassy at three o'clock, had her hair done by an Italian stylist at four o'clock, and was ready at five o'clock for a tour of the Vatican and a meeting with the pope, a quick-change schedule that amused and amazed the Italians. For the Vatican meeting, Barbara wore a black suit by Arnold Scaasi. She had to go to a dressy dinner immediately afterward, but that was no problem clothes-wise—she simply took off the suit jacket to reveal a lacy white top.

She told her staff she wanted to stop in at Ferragamo's, a top Italian shoemaker, but she didn't have time, and in fact didn't do any shopping on the trip. "I'm not a good shopper," she said. "I'm a good sightseer."

Sightseeing yielded one surprise in Italy. George Bush made a spot decision to visit the USS *Guadalcanal* off Anzio Beach, and during the tour Barbara ran into a startled seaman who was just getting out of the shower—wrapped only in a towel.[5]

In Belgium Barbara went to gala luncheons, concerts, and dinners, but she also visited a village outside Brussels that was built especially for the mentally handicapped, one of five such government-subsidized towns in the country for adults capable of living semi-independently under supervision.

"It's an absolutely wonderful project," Barbara said. When she arrived, two residents presented her with flowers, then she was taken on a tour to see the many workshops in the village—candles, baked goods, and fabrics all produced and sold to the public in a competitive market.

As Barbara was getting ready to leave the village, she was given a gift by one of the residents, a twenty-year-old woman named Beatrice, who had made a puppetlike witch on a broomstick for the First Lady. Having presented the gift, Beatrice began to cry from the emotion of it all. When Barbara realized what had happened, she went over and patted the young woman on the shoulder. "I wish I could say what I really feel in French," Barbara said. "But all I can say is *merci beaucoup.*"

She made another remark on her lack of formal education when visiting the library at the University of Leuven. "I was a terrible student," she said, referring to her single year at Smith College. "I'm a late bloomer."

The highlight of the European tour was London, where Barbara stole the spotlight by spontaneously reaching for the hand of Denis Thatcher and planting a big kiss on it.

The incident occurred as Barbara arrived at 10 Downing Street to join her husband, who had been meeting with Prime Minister Margaret Thatcher. Denis Thatcher greeted Barbara with a kiss on the hand, but some photographers missed the shot and asked for a repeat of the kiss. At that point, Barbara reached quickly for Denis Thatcher's hand instead. This time all the photographers got the picture, and it ran in newspapers all over the world.

Earlier in the day Barbara had toured Brixton, a poor immigrant neighborhood in London. She stopped in at an adult education center to see how the English cope with illiteracy and talked with students from Angola, Ghana, Ethiopia, and Zaire as well as with school officials. She told them that in some places in the United States "there are enormous waiting lists for literacy. It's heartbreaking."

In a lighter moment, she joined in a cooking class that was making strudel, which she said she had not made before, adding: "My pie crust is nothing to write home about."

At the school's day-care center, the children presented Barbara with a brightly colored paper teapot, which inspired her to recite an English nursery rhyme.

"I'm a little teapot short and stout. Here is my handle, here is my spout," she sang, extending her left arm as a spout.

"Do you know it?" she asked the three-year-olds. They looked bewildered but the grown-ups smiled in appreciation.

Barbara went several rungs up the social ladder after leaving Brixton. Lunch that day was at Buckingham Palace. George took her hand as the photographers snapped their pictures. Queen Elizabeth's staff served salmon mousse, duck, asparagus, and, for dessert, mango ice cream.

That night the Bushes wound up their weeklong, 9,000-mile journey at a dinner given by the Thatchers. When they got home, they went straight to Kennebunkport for a rest.

Just five weeks later, however, another European trip was scheduled, with stops in Poland, Hungary, Paris, and the Netherlands. Barbara, having learned from the rigors of the last trip, decided to pack more clothes this time—"just everything in my closet"—and to have a fresh outfit for every appearance.

On the previous trip, she said, she had forgotten that the president's wife is widely photographed each time she gets on a plane and gets off.

"I forgot that of course you can't just throw on something and get on an airplane and then change your clothes on the plane," she said. "You've got to be seen getting on and off."

With careful planning that took several days, she filled a hanging bag with clothes for each of the four countries she would be visiting. Having gone to so much trouble, she joked with reporters about her efforts. "I hope you have noticed," she said. "I've killed myself."

Her husband, she said, did his own packing as usual and got through the job in about twenty minutes. He even packed two tuxedos on the advice of an aide, in case he spilled something on one of them.

The first stop was Poland, a country full of excitement over the Solidarity movement and the retreat of communism. In Warsaw the Bushes gave a luncheon at the U.S. ambassador's residence, mixing longtime Communist leaders with major figures from Solidarity. Barbara's table included both Communist Party leader Wojciech Jaruzelski and Solidarity's chief spokesman, Janusz Onyszkiewicz, who emphasized how much Poland had changed. "If you take into account that a year ago I was in prison it was rather strange," he said.

Barbara later said that she had found Jaruzelski nothing like the stone-faced Communist he often seemed in public appearances. When George Bush invited the men at the luncheon to take off their coats, she said, Jaruzelski told her he would have to sneak out and take off his suspenders as well. Later, when he stood up to give a toast, he joked, "Well, I better be careful. I've gotta remember I don't have my suspenders on."

That night Jaruzelski held a dinner for the Bushes and also invited many Solidarity and Catholic Church leaders. Barbara, making good on her clothes promise, changed from the navy and white cotton she had worn during the day to a spectacular red-flowered dress for the evening. Outside the dinner, held at a seventeenth-century palace, demonstrators shouted, "May Bush live one hundred years" and "Down with Communism." Bush, in his toast, said, "Poland is entering a new era. It is beginning once again to command its own destiny."

Before leaving Warsaw, George Bush presented a gift to the Polish people—Little League charters and enough uniforms and baseball equipment for ten Little League teams. "Perhaps nothing is more American than Little League baseball," he said. "Well, few things show America's love for Poland like bringing our national pastime to you."

The next day the Bushes flew to Gdansk to have lunch with Solidarity leader Lech Walesa, who in later years would replace Jaruzelski as head of Poland's government.

Walesa and his wife Danuta lived in a two-story stucco house. Even though it was a modest dwelling, Walesa said he was able to buy it only because of payments he got from Solidarity. "If I were an ordinary Pole, I would not be able to afford it," he said.

Lunch was substantial and rich—salmon, eel, a cold vegetable soup, turkey, roast beef, schnitzel, and pork loin with Jell-O for dessert.

Bush, who drank a small glass of vodka with the lunch, ate heartily. "My mother taught me to eat what's before you," he said. "In this house, I would weigh three hundred pounds."

After lunch, the Walesas took the Bushes to the Solidarity Workers Monument. Huge crowds lined the roads along the way, singing a traditional Polish song, "One Hundred Years." George, Barbara, and Lech Walesa all got out of the limousine to shake hands. It was a moving, emotional experience for everyone involved, Americans and Poles, sharing a realization that democracy was taking hold in a country long ruled by communism.

Barbara said later that Walesa kept saying "Oh my gosh, oh my gosh, oh fantastic, fantastic." She added, "I'm sort of cleaning up the 'oh my goshes,' but it really was exciting."

Recalling her last visit to Poland in 1987, Barbara said, "I think there was an awful lot of hope that we did not see the last time, an enormous amount of hope tempered with a little bit of caution."

During the stop in Gdansk, Barbara went out on her own only once, with Jaruzelski's wife Barbara to the town hall in Gdansk. Her schedule called for a stroll around the building to look at its medieval architecture, but crowds near the structure were so enthusiastic that security guards got nervous and sent her straight inside instead. Barbara said later that she had noticed major changes in the Polish leader's wife—she had lost considerable weight and learned English since the Bushes' last visit to Poland.

"She was always lovely but I said, 'I just can't get over how thin you are.' She told us that she wanted her husband to get out of politics. I don't know if that's true or not, but they were just much more open, much more open."

In Hungary, the next stop on the European tour, Barbara played a more substantial role, visiting a camp the Hungarians had set up to accept Romanians fleeing from the despised government of Nicolae Ceausescu, who would later be vengefully executed by his own people.

The refugee settlement, located on an island outside of Budapest, was set up by Hungarian lawyer Ferenc Janka to protect ethnic Hungarians from the Transylvania area controlled by Romania. The five hundred refugees described a society intent on eradicating their culture—one young woman said authorities had tried to force her to change her baby's name.

Barbara met many of the families and got her hand kissed many times in traditional European fashion. "I have often thought the worst thing that could happen to you would be to have your country taken away from you," she said. "And the second worst thing would be to have no one accept you in their country with loving arms."

One couple at the settlement said that the Bush visit to Hungary at a time when it was opening its borders would irritate Romania, which was closing its own borders tighter than ever. "For people back in Romania, it tells them that reforms are under way in Hungary and that George Bush is here to point up those reforms," they said.

As Barbara left the camp, the refugees presented her with a blue glass vase that had George Bush's face appliquéd in paper. Looking at the vase, Barbara murmured, "Good-looking man."

She also visited a center for handicapped children run by the Catholic Church in Budapest. Eleven of the children sang and recited a biblical skit for her and her companion, Erzsbet Nemeth, wife of the Hungarian prime minister. Mrs. Nemeth broke into tears during the performance. Barbara wrote in the guest book, "I feel God's love in this wonderful house. God bless you all. Thank you for letting me share in this great moment. I will care more, thanks to you."

That night the Bushes hosted a party for the Hungarians. As in Poland, it was a mix of Communists and leaders from the opposition parties. A Hungarian band played country and western music, but the ambassador flew in American shrimp for the occasion.

Afterward, on the flight to Paris, Barbara said she had been especially impressed by the changes in Hungary since her last visit in 1983. Poland, she said, had always had "enormous pride and spirit, more than any other Eastern European country I'd ever been in, so I wasn't surprised to see it again. Just more so. But Hungary, I think, has changed enormously since we were there."

When the Bushes arrived in Paris, they found it in a festive mood celebrating the 200th anniversary of the French revolution and also hosting an economic summit for the seven major industrial nations.

Barbara began by attending a luncheon given by Danielle Mitterrand, wife of the French leader. Afterward she went to the Louvre and then to the American Hospital in Paris to unveil a plaque dedicating a new wing. Engraved on the plaque was a notation that Barbara Bush had dedicated the hospital wing "on the occasion of the visit to Paris of George Bush."

Barbara, recalling that George had torn up his speech in Budapest and given a short talk instead to a rain-soaked crowd, decided to do the same at the hospital dedication.

"I'm going to show you that I learned something from my husband in Hungary," she said. "I'm going to give up my speech and just tell you that speaking from the heart, as he did, this is one of the nicest things that ever could happen to me and selfishly, I feel like you've stretched my life a little bit because now I'm on a plaque."

She also stopped in the hospital for a visit, talking with a man who had developed acute appendicitis while visiting Paris and telling a retired surgeon who was from New York City, "So am I, but don't tell anybody. Don't tell them down in Texas."

Besides the plaque with her name on it, Barbara received another surprise from the Parisians—a rose that will always bear her name. Cross-bred to get a red and white color, it was planted in the Bagatelle rose garden in the Bois de Boulogne in Paris, which includes strains of roses named after many famous people, including John Kennedy and Princess Grace of Monaco.

But the Barbara Bush rose was the first named after the wife of an American president. Barbara was presented with a large bouquet by Bernadette Chirac, wife of the mayor of Paris.

"It's almost like having a baby," Barbara said, sniffing the roses. "I feel like a grandmother with a new child. They'll still be here when I'm gone. I adore them. I love the color combination."

Horticulturist Henri Delbard, who developed the rose, also promised Barbara a bush of the flowers for the White House Rose Garden. "We'll have to plant it," she said.

The Paris trip included numerous luncheons and dinners. Barbara found that her hosts didn't follow her own practice of breaking protocol occasionally to make sure that foreign guests aren't seated next to the same person meal after meal.

"I have now become glued to Mr. Mobutu," she said, referring to the president of Zaire who was her dinner companion a number of times. "I teased him because he doesn't eat vegetables and I told him when he comes [to the United States] I'm going to only give him regular water and artichokes because he certainly doesn't drink regular water and he certainly does not touch artichokes."[6]

The last visit on the European tour was the Netherlands, where Barbara unveiled another permanent structure marked with her name. This one was the cornerstone of the American School of the Hague, which had just began construction. The stone read, "This cornerstone unveiled by Mrs. Barbara Bush, first lady, July 17, 1989, on the occasion of the first visit by a president of the United States of America."

But perhaps the most interesting stop during the short visit was at a church in Leiden, where President Bush gave a speech and then learned from the mayor that two of the Bush family's ancestors had lived in the city and sailed on the

Mayflower to America in 1620. Mayor Cornelis Goekoop told Bush that Francis Cooke, a signer of the Mayflower Compact, and Hester De La Noye, had a daughter named Jane, who was Bush's "grandmother" eleven generations back. The mayor said that Hester's sister Marie had a child named Philippe, whose grandchild—seven times removed— was Franklin Delano Roosevelt. "Two sisters, two presidents," Mayor Goekoop said.

The trip was a success from Barbara's point of view, exhilarating, but also tiring. While George had jogged every day, "bless his heart," and had gained no weight despite the rich meals, she hadn't done any exercise.

"I could have but I've been sort of tired," she said. "I've been trying to keep my diary up and my thank-you letters in the spare time and so I've sort of been a slug. But I'm up to date, so that's not bad."

Barbara returned to Europe many more times during George Bush's first term in the White House, traveling with her husband, seeing many of the same world leaders again.

She made only one major trip without the president—in May 1990 to Costa Rica, where she represented the United States at the inauguration of President Rafael Calderón. It was her first trip to Costa Rica and her first time heading a diplomatic mission. Her support crew included Spanish-speaking son Jeb, a friend of the Calderóns, and White House Chief of Staff John Sununu.

The trip got off to a late start because Barbara—uncharacteristically—left the White House and then realized she had forgotten one of her two suitcases. She had to go back to get it.

She also noted ruefully that almost everyone in the delegation except her spoke Spanish.

Barbara carried a letter from President Bush to Calderón that wished him well. At the bottom, Bush had written by hand, "Barbara, Jeb and Columba are thrilled to be with you on this great day." But Columba, Jeb's Mexican-born wife, had to cancel at the last minute because their son was sick.

When she arrived at the airport in Costa Rica, Barbara was met by outgoing President Oscar Arias Sanchez. "Our main purpose for being in San José is to join all Costa Ricans in celebrating those most precious democratic activities—the recognition of the will of the people, the rule of law and the peaceful participation of all citizens in the selection of their leaders," she said.

At the inaugural ceremonies, she got more applause than any other delegation leader except Violeta Chamorro, who had recently been elected president of Nicaragua, knocking the leftist Sandinistas from power.

Before the ceremony, Barbara had breakfast with Calderón, his mother, his wife Gloria, and their four children at the family's home. "I just fell in love with them and asked them to come live with me forever," she said afterward. "But unfortunately, they declined."

Calderón predicted that Barbara would be warmly welcomed at the ceremony. "Our wives are more popular than we are," he said.

Barbara, picking up on the line and perhaps recognizing a hint of condescension, looked with amusement at Gloria Calderón. "How come we're not presidents?" she said.

While she appeared to enjoy her solo trip, Barbara emphasized that she would not make a habit of it, and she stuck to her policy of not talking about major political questions.

"Nobody said, 'Don't speak about politics, Bar,' " she said, then paused. "Nobody was right."

But whether she is traveling alone or with George Bush, Barbara puts a lot of effort into making a good impression abroad. She enjoys the historic nature of the journeys and understands what a privilege it is to represent the United States all over the globe.

"Imagine knowing heads of every country, on a fairly personal basis in many cases," she said. "Or imagine traveling to all those foreign countries. I feel like I have had the best, the most exciting, thrilling life anyone could ever have."

A Helping Hand

*B*arbara Bush was watching a rock star on a TV talk show. He was telling the interviewer that he had made millions of dollars in Britain.

"What did you do with all that money?" the interviewer asked.

"Well, I think I sniffed it up my nose, ha ha ha," the rock star replied. The reporter joined in the laughter.

Barbara failed to see the humor. As the rock star and the well-paid reporter sat there laughing, all she could think about were the rows and rows of damaged babies she had seen in hospitals around the country. Their parents had also sniffed drugs up their noses ha, ha, ha, she thought angrily.

"We've got to stop having someone on television say, 'I sniffed it all up, ha, ha, ha,' and having the reporter laugh," she said. ". . . We cannot have television showing role models of people doing things which are wrong. I just was shocked . . . I just couldn't believe that was on. They were all laughing away at it.

"We've got to stand up and say, 'Enough!' "[1]

Coming from some public figures, such a statement might seem hypocritical. They visit hospitals in election years, make a show of cuddling a sick baby or holding the hand of an elderly patient, but have little interest in such problems once they get into office.

Barbara had earned the right to speak out. She started volunteering in hospitals long before she became famous. She did the kind of work—even emptying bedpans—that gave her up-close experience with many patients.

With five children, she was busy at home, but as George Bush's oil business prospered she was able to hire household help. While she didn't have a paying job, she put her energy into charity work. Her friends are unanimous in saying that when she decided to join a cause, she actually worked on it—she was never just a name on the masthead.

By the time George Bush became vice president, Barbara estimated that she was spending 50 percent of her time on volunteer work. With her higher profile, much of the work shifted from hands-on help to showcasing good causes, especially reading. She joined the national board of Reading is Fundamental and became a sponsor of another literacy group, Laubach Literacy International, and she traveled all over the country to get people to focus on the issue.

Sometimes she had a wide audience. In 1987, for example, she appeared on an ABC-TV Fourth of July special celebrating the bicentennial of the U.S. Constitution. Her part in the show was to introduce sixty-three-year-old former sharecropper J. T. Pace, a South Carolina man who had learned to read just a year earlier. His job was to read the preamble to the Constitution during the dramatic finale.

The program was to be broadcast live from St. Louis, and Pace was to meet the vice president's wife there for the first time. As show time approached, however, he got nervous, telling producer Vince Maynard that he didn't understand all the words in the preamble and that he couldn't go on with the show. The producer tried to change his mind, but without success. Finally Maynard suggested that Pace talk with Barbara Bush anyway. Pace agreed.

Barbara, using what her brother Scott calls her "spectacular people skills," was able to empathize with the former sharecropper. She told him that she sometimes had difficulty with big words herself, in fact all readers did. She kept on talking for a while and then took the man's hands.

"What if you and I read the preamble together?" she asked. Pace smiled. "I'd like that," he said.[2]

When the time came, the two of them stood at the podium side by side and began reading. Pace stumbled on some of the more difficult words at first, but his confidence grew as he talked and Barbara Bush's voice faded into the background.

"We the People of the United States, in order to form a more perfect union, establish justice, insure domestic tranquility, provide for the common defense, promote the general welfare and secure the blessings of liberty to ourselves and our posterity, do ordain and establish this Constitution for the United States of America."

When Pace finished he and Barbara Bush embraced and the audience gave them a standing ovation.

The ABC show had an emotional impact on millions of TV viewers, but more often Barbara's literacy work was on a smaller, less showy scale. Typically, during the vice presidential years, she would appear at a local school where children were being honored for reading a certain number of books, or to present a check to officials for programs designed to improve reading skills or to get parents more involved in the education of their children.

She also cited her own childhood experiences to interest children in reading. "We all read aloud as youngsters," she told grade schoolers in Alexandria, Virginia, in 1981. "Our favorites were the Oz books. My brother got the whole set, the lucky duck."

By 1983 the *Washington Post* had run more than one editorial praising Barbara for the work she was doing in reading and the attention she had brought to the cause of illiteracy.

"She is much more than a fancy name on a charity letterhead," the *Post* said, referring to her success in raising money that provided more than 200,000 books to Washington schools. "The beauty of this program as well as the contribution of Mrs. Bush is in its directness—no endless series of planning meetings or busy work, no splashy annual appearance at a fancy 'do,' but face to face, on the scene help that delivers immediate, visible results."[3]

Besides appearing at numerous schools and literacy events, Barbara talked up the issue with other people who could do something about it. Harold McGraw, retired from the publishing firm McGraw-Hill, credits a dinner party conversation he had with Barbara as his inspiration for starting a business council on literacy. She agreed to be on the board of directors after he got it going.

"I believe if we can lick the problem of people being functionally illiterate—unable to read or write at the fifth-grade level—we will then go on to solve most of the other major problems besetting this country," she said.

By 1985, she told an audience in Los Angeles, she had given more than three hundred speeches on adult literacy alone, and the issue was seeping into the consciousness of more and more Americans.

"I do it every day . . . and the media is wonderful about reporting it," she said. "You probably don't hear about it here, but in Topeka, Kansas, I was very big. It gets out."

While schools and civic groups were her main audiences, Barbara also spoke at prisons, sometimes with amusing results. "She once told me that she met a guy who had been in prison for stealing," nephew Jamie Bush reported. "She went to a literacy program for prisoners and the man told her his story. He got caught because he couldn't read the exit sign on the door of the supermarket he was robbing."

"She urged him to develop his reading skills—and then put them to good use!"[4]

During the 1988 presidential campaign, Barbara continued to talk about literacy, but she also put more emphasis on programs designed to help the disabled, the poor, and the homeless.

In Enid, Oklahoma, she sat at a workshop for the retarded, listening to a young woman describe her efforts to find a job. With crowds of onlookers and cameras around her, the woman began to stammer. Barbara immediately leaned over and put a hand on the woman's arm. "Are you nervous with all the cameras?" she asked. The woman nodded, happy to get the problem out in the open, and she was able to continue with her story.

Staying in hotels all over the country, Barbara realized that the management put much more soap in each room than any visitor was likely to use, and she began to take the extra bars with her. When she got enough, she gave them to a homeless shelter.

"I share with George the information I gather about the homeless," she said. "In fact, he teases me when I take soap and shampoo from hotels to send to women's shelters. For instance, when we stay in a hotel, we are given five bars of soap. George and I share one and I send the other four to the shelters so each woman can have her own soap."[5]

Barbara's charity work has been praised by Democrats and Republicans as nonpartisan, but during the heat of the '88 campaign, politics loomed over the good works.

In New Orleans she visited a day-care center for both adults and children funded with federal, state, and private funds—the kind of mix favored by George Bush. Before she got inside, however, she had to walk past angry, sign-carrying women and youths complaining that the Republican administration had not done enough for them. "For the past eight years, where was George when the poor people needed him," one sign said, picking up a theme from the Democratic political convention. Barbara ignored the protesters and went inside to talk as planned.

In the daily column she wrote for *USA Today* during the campaign, Barbara often wrote of the good works she had visited, and sometimes her remarks had a distinctly partisan overtone.

"What I really want to write about this week are the thou-

sand points of light George talked about at the convention,"
she said in an October 3 column. "I saw them everywhere I
went and through the people I met."[6]

She described two day-care centers, one run with private
money and the other federally funded. "Both centers have
professional and volunteer staff," she said. "Both are different programs and, under George's child-care plan, the parents would get to choose which one their child attends."

Barbara also lauded two programs run almost entirely by
volunteers and praised a city—Hot Springs, Arkansas—that
was being renovated with a mix of government and private
funds.

The "points of light" theme ran through Barbara's initial
charitable outings once she got in the White House as well.
Her first trip, two weeks after she became First Lady, was to
Martha's Table a few blocks from the White House, a non-
profit group that uses volunteers to distribute donated food
to the homeless and also provides meals at an after-school
center for children.

Her half-hour visit to the center drew fifty reporters and
camera crews. She took along a box of cookies made at the
White House and a book to read to the children—*How
Fletcher Was Hatched*. But she stopped first to talk with volunteers who make 1,700 sandwiches each day for delivery to
homeless men and women. While she talked, Barbara put on
a red apron, washed her hands on a towelette, and made
eight meat and cheese sandwiches.

She said she had chosen Martha's Table for her first outing
"because I'm hoping Americans will look at this range of
volunteers and realize how important it is, what a job they do
and how really important it is to help people who need some
help."

When she got to the children's room, she quickly com-
manded attention, telling the thirty-five children, "Everybody quiet. Everybody sit down please." She read the story,
about a dog hatched from an egg, in a lively manner, frequently turning the book toward the children so they could

see the pictures. "This is the longest book," she said at one point.

Afterward, she asked the children questions about the story and got them to howl like dogs.

Did she want to know their names? one child asked. She did. And they told her.

A few days later Barbara visited a thrift shop in suburban Virginia, another privately run organization that helps poor families. She brought along seven plastic bags of clothes and toys as a donation and talked with the people who ran the program. Later she told reporters, "You know, I don't think anybody realizes—or I didn't realize—that 70 percent of the people who are helping are working poor."

Philadelphia was chosen as the site of Barbara's first out-of-town appearance as First Lady, thanks to persistent invitations from Sheila Whitelaw, executive director of the city's Friends of the Free Library, who said she began her campaign in early December, let up around Christmas, then resumed her effort before the inauguration. "The next thing I knew, they called me," she said with delight.

Barbara's book of the day was *Alexander and the Terrible, Horrible, No Good, Very Bad Day,* by Judith Viorst. The grade school children who heard the story joined in the refrain with the First Lady: "I could tell it was going to be a terrible, horrible, no good, very bad day."

On Valentine's Day, Barbara visited a place that had long ago won her heart—the Washington Home and Hospice, a long-term care facility. Accustomed to her visits, which started shortly after George Bush was elected to Congress in 1966, the residents wanted to know what life was like in the White House.

Barbara told them about the inaugural and how her own grown children had celebrated—some of them all night long.

"Some of those children of ours had danced till three or four in the morning so they were not just a lot of fun at breakfast," she said. "But the grandchildren—we had ten in the house—they came in and climbed on the bed and played. And we did have a wonderful time."

The residents gave her a giant Valentine inscribed ALWAYS THE FIRST LADY IN OUR HEARTS, and she had cards for each of them as well. "I really mean, I love you all," she told a group of elderly men and women who surrounded her with their wheelchairs.[7]

A few weeks before Valentine's Day, Barbara had recorded an appeal to Washington residents for donations and Valentines for the city's abused children. Local radio stations picked up the tape and ran it during prime commuting hours. The result was more than 10,000 Valentines delivered to Children's Hospital in the city and donations totaling more than $140,000. The money was split between the hospital and the local chapter of Childhelp USA, which named Barbara as national honorary chairman for the year.

"The impact on the morale of campaign workers was just tremendous," said Richard Tubbs, director of the Have A Heart campaign. "It's the best you can find in America when she took the time to reach out."

A couple of days later, Barbara flew to Denver to see her newest grandchild, ten-day-old Ashley Walker Bush, daughter of Neil and Sharon Bush. But after she landed at the airport, her first stop was at the Food Bank of the Rockies, an organization that distributes supplies to groups which help feed the needy. Son Neil joined his mother at the Food Bank, then took her home to meet the baby.

The next day, back in Washington, Barbara spotlighted an elementary school in a depressed area of the city as part of a celebration of Black History Month. Student Milton Law, who gave a dramatic recitation of Martin Luther King's "I Have a Dream" speech, said later he was impressed to see Barbara Bush swaying with the glee club and singing "We Shall Overcome." She knew all six verses.

In early March educators, publishers, and community and business leaders were invited to a White House luncheon for the formation of the Barbara Bush Foundation for Family

Literacy. She told the audience she had already received commitments of $1 million for the foundation, which would be privately run, and she would serve as honorary chairman.

The idea was to develop programs that helped entire families with reading problems—the adults as well as children:

"In ten years of traveling around the United States of America visiting literary programs, libraries, kindergarten groups, day-care centers, single-parent classes for high school dropouts, public housing projects, food banks—you name it, I've visited it—it has become very apparent to me that we must attack the problem of a more literate America through the family," Barbara said. "We all know of adults with reading problems tending to raise children with reading problems."

President Bush dropped in on the gathering to support his wife's effort. "I'm the observer, I'm the fly on the wall in this project and as interested as anybody in this room," he said. "I've studied with Barbara Bush on the importance of all of this and I've learned a lot."

The luncheon drew 120 guests, including three young children who were cited as success stories from various literacy programs. One of them, three-year-old Felecia Fennell of Fayetteville, North Carolina, sat in a high chair and babbled happily throughout the event.

Later Barbara was asked why she was putting so much emphasis on family literacy instead of concentrating on individuals.

"I've visited a lot of Project Head Starts and they're wonderful," she said. "But they really aren't as wonderful as they could be because, in many cases, they're not working with the mothers and fathers. That's one thing that sort of got me. I mean I could have had just a Barbara Bush Foundation for Literacy but in the last three or four years it has come to me that the family is what makes the difference.

"The home is the child's first school. The parent is the child's first teacher. Reading is the child's first subject."[8]

Barbara's emphasis on family learning led her to seek out examples of programs that cater to the idea. One of them was All Children's House in New York City, where pre-school children of the affluent mingle with those from poor and homeless families.

One of the mothers on hand for Barbara's visit was a school dropout working to get a high school equivalency degree from a special program at her son's elementary school. "The people here encourage us all to go to school," she said.

The staff director, Gretchen Buchenholz, said, "Children of all backgrounds benefit by just being kids here together. But for children who come from unstable families, you have to reach out to their parents. Our program can be replicated and collateral services can be extended into school grades. That's what I hope Barbara Bush sees."

A few months after Barbara started her literacy foundation, she got a big boost—Kind Fahd of Saudi Arabia contributed $1 million.

Among the highlights of Barbara's early months in the White House was a visit in March to Grandma's House, a Washington home for four abandoned babies infected with the AIDS virus. At the time, many Americans believed that the virus could be spread just by touching an infected person. Barbara's mission was to demonstrate that fear was unfounded.

She cradled an infected infant, kissed a lively twenty-month-old toddler, and hugged an adult AIDS victim. Volunteers who work with AIDS patients were overjoyed at the image, played in newspapers across the country, of the First Lady hugging a baby with the AIDS virus.

"You can't imagine what one hug from the First Lady is worth," said Jim Graham, administrator of a clinic that treats AIDS patients. "We've had so much trouble with all the talk about the dangers of personal contact. Here the First Lady isn't afraid—and that's worth more than a thousand public service announcements."[9]

Indeed, Barbara's visit to Grandma's House resulted in a huge number of calls from people volunteering both time and money.

As Barbara left the house, she said she wanted "to make a big push for not doing drugs. Many of those who test positive are the children of intravenous drug users—and that's terrible."

On Mother's Day, she visited a Ronald McDonald's House in Washington, part of a privately funded national network that provides housing for families who must travel out of town to treat a sick child.

"It makes an enormous difference to have a beautiful house where other people know what's happening to you," she said. "This particular house has sixty volunteers without whom it couldn't run at all. They need more volunteers. They need money—and it just gives something to people who have a tragedy."

Then, noting that the house had a plaque describing the Bushes' loss of three-year-old Robin, Barbara, on the verge of tears, said, "I'm going to try and tell you that Robin's name is in this house—and I like that very much."

She might have said more. But as often happens when she talks about the daughter who died of leukemia, Barbara got teary-eyed and had to turn away from the TV cameras.

Despite her emphasis on the importance of volunteers, Barbara has made clear that she is aware the best social programs also have strong, paid staffs.

"The meat of the program really is the professional," she said. "And you need money for that. You have to have the professionals who put everything in place and keep the program going and keep the volunteers coming in."

While she successfully solicits millions of dollars in private contributions, she said, she leaves it to elected officials to decide how many tax dollars to provide for each needy cause.

"I have never lobbied my husband—with a few exceptions," she said.

In the spring of 1989, Barbara was invited to dozens of

colleges as commencement speaker. She chose a small black women's school in North Carolina for her first outing and also agreed to speak at the college she had attended for one year—Smith, where she was to get an honorary degree.

The choice of Bennett College in Greensboro, North Carolina, site of a famous sit-in during the civil rights movement of the 1960s, was designed to highlight Barbara's commitment to equal rights for American blacks. But most of those at the ceremony didn't seem much concerned about symbolism. Parents and students alike were just glad that graduation day had at last arrived, and they considered the First Lady's visit to be icing on the cake.

"God, how I've waited for this day. It's been a long, hard time. I couldn't be happier," said Yvonne Roberson, whose daughter Michelle was getting a degree in health sciences—the first member of the family to receive a college degree. Having Barbara Bush as speaker is "giving me another chill," Roberson said. "It's about the best honor we could have."

Some of the graduating seniors saw a practical benefit as well. "She's putting Bennett on the map," said twenty-three-year-old Regina Hucks. "They're going to know all about us when we go for job interviews."[10]

In her speech Barbara talked about people, including Frederick Douglass, who had learned to read against all odds and gone on to greatness.

"I can't tell you all the people I've known who have escaped the bondage of ignorance," she said. "You graduates have recognized this. And I urge you to help the young out there today . . . enslaved by ignorance."

The Smith visit was also an emotional one for Barbara. She told the graduates she had no regrets about leaving college after one year to get married at age nineteen and have a baby, but lamented that her father was not still alive to see her finally get a degree—even an honorary one.

Later she told reporters she thinks it is important for young women to get a college degree—"very important. I think most women would not have been as lucky as I was—but remember, we're talking about forty-five years ago."

She also urged students to put off childbearing until they complete their education. "I'm saying to young women, 'Wait, you've got years to have a family.' "

Then, realizing how all this advice conflicted with her own example, Barbara grinned. "It sounds like 'Do as I don't,' " she said.

For every visit Barbara made, she turned down many others. She visited a center for runaways in New York City, listening to the sad tales of young survivors of the streets. She decided not to appear on an episode of TV's *Golden Girls* to promote the Special Olympics, feeling it was inappropriate for her to be seen in a comedy. But she read a story to Big Bird, Count von Count, and five preschoolers on *Sesame Street*.

Barbara's heavily publicized good works inspired many Americans to write and ask how they could get involved in her projects. She replied that a much better alternative was for them to find someone who needed help in their own communities. "Walk out your door and help someone," she said. "Whether you help them in the library or whether you adopt a school and are a volunteer in the public school, whether you go to a shelter and help somebody, whether you go volunteer in a hospital—whatever you do, you're helping me."

She said she realized that many people have very busy lives. But she added, "Everybody has something, whether you have time or money or know-how or space. Today you can no longer say, 'The drug problem worries me,' or 'Crime worries me' or 'Illiteracy worries me.' If it worries you, then you've got to do something about it."[11]

Traveling around the country, seeing so many people involved in helping others, inspires her. She said she senses that more people are feeling a sense of social responsibility and that many Americans are able to use their neighborhoods as extended families, much as she and George Bush did when they were a young couple without any nearby family in Texas.

"I sense that young people are beginning to think in terms of extended family again," she said. "The extended families may not even be related. They may be neighbors, friends. People are saying, 'What affects me affects my neighbors.' When problems arise—crime, drugs, bad schools—each person says, 'This isn't good. I have to do something about it.' "[12]

Barbara also used her high profile and popularity to urge women to take care of themselves. She was the guest speaker when the National Cancer Institute launched a campaign to make women more aware of the dangers of breast cancer and how mammograms can lead to early detection and life-saving intervention.

"As you know, three of my predecessors—Happy Rockefeller, Betty Ford, and Nancy Reagan—faced the challenge of breast cancer," she said. "At a time when their lives were so public these three shared with us all their private battles." (Less than a year later, Barbara herself would have surgery to remove a small cancer from her lip.)

Because breast cancer strikes one in ten American women, she said, all women over forty should have regular mammograms. "Pick up the phone and make a life-saving appointment," she said.

She urged women who work to give their children priority—and asked that employers be accommodating as well.

"It's hard on you but you have to put your children first," she said. "And I think your boss has to accommodate a little bit. I mean, if you need to go to school to see your child in a school situation, they should make accommodations for it. You'll have to make it up, but that's just a fact of life."

During her first Christmas season in the White House, Barbara did several good deeds. The one that drew the most attention involved the Salvation Army, which for years has had bell ringers stationed outside stores and at malls, asking for donations for the needy. Some malls in 1989 decided the bell ringers were a nuisance—even though they never pressed anyone for a donation—and banned them. The Washington director of the Salvation Army estimated the decision would cost the army about $100,000.

When Barbara read about the ban, she sought out a mall that still allowed the bell ringers, pointedly dropped a ten-dollar bill in the kettle, and told the Salvation Army volunteer Evelyn Barnes how much she liked the charity.

"I'm a great fan of the Salvation Army," she said. "I wanted to tell you what great work you're doing."

Publicity about the incident inspired a local business to give the Salvation Army $100,000.

Barbara also dropped in at the Central Union Mission, a charity that has been around for more than one hundred years and now helps needy mothers, serves meals to the homeless, distributes clothes, and provides shelter. Mothers with young children crowded into the center for the visit, and Barbara read the Christmas story from the Bible.

"This is a good story," she told the children, "so good it lasted almost 2,000 years." Afterward she and the mothers and a few of the children sang "Away in a Manger."

Robert Rich, the mission director, said the shelter offered a weekly program for preschoolers while their mothers take classes on finding and maintaining a home. "For a lot of these women, the name of the game is survival," he said.

During the rest of her first term in the White House, Barbara followed a similar schedule, always keeping her primary emphasis on literacy. In the fall of 1990 her family literacy group gave out awards totaling $500,000 to public and private groups that target what Barbara called an "intergenerational cycle of illiteracy."

In October that year she wrote an article for *Reader's Digest* offering advice to parents and others who read aloud to children, based on her own experience with five children, twelve grandchildren, and numerous sessions in schools and libraries around the country. Here are excerpts:

1. Get started now. You can't begin too soon.

2. Make reading aloud a habit. Years ago, I usually read to my children at bedtime. Most evenings we'd snuggle together with a few favorite books. The kids came to love this special time. They learned passages from their favorite books by heart, which we'd recite together. It doesn't matter when you read but it is helpful to do it at the same time each day, for at least fifteen minutes. Over twenty years ago, University of Illinois researcher Dolores Durkin studied 205 children who learned to read before starting school. They had one thing in common: Their parents made reading to them a habit.

3. Involve the whole family. Children enjoy being read to by people besides their mothers. Many people read to me when I was little: my father, a brother, a grandmother, even friends barely older than I. Today, both parents often work and may not be able to read as frequently as they'd like. Baby sitters, child care providers, and older siblings can sometimes help by reading to their charges. George doesn't get much chance to read to our grandchildren in Washington but he does better when we're in Kennebunkport. Each morning at six o'clock, the grandchildren race into our room, bounce into bed with us, and wave their favorite books. Often it's George who begins our morning reading time. Children like it when the men in their family read to them. Educators hear this over and over around the country. When a girl in elementary school chose a book on football, her teacher asked why. "My dad likes football," the student explained.

4. Keep books handy. Research shows that growing up in a house filled with books often helps children become an early reader. For my grandchildren, I keep stacks of books at Camp David, at Kennebunkport, and at the White House. There are Bible stories, Barbara Cooney's *Miss Rumphius,* Martin Handford's picture book *Where's Waldo?* and several nearly worn-out copies of *Old Mother West Wind* stories by Thornton W. Burgess, which I treasured as a

child. A home library need not be expensive. Low-priced children's books are available even in supermarkets. You can watch for garage sales, trade books with other families, and ask relatives to give books as gifts. The best bargain, of course, is at the country's 15,000 public libraries.

5. Choosing good books. Children need books appropriate for their interests, their ages, and their ability, educators say. They also need variety, so experts suggest we read different things to our children—newspapers, magazines, streetsigns, even the backs of cereal boxes. That way we show the importance of words in every aspect of life. Youngsters love to hear the same stories over and over. I read Robert McCloskey's *Make Way for Ducklings* so many times to my children and grandchildren that the book fell apart. Repetition improves vocabulary and memory and helps children understand how stories work.

6. Make the written word come alive. In reading to my children and grandchildren, I always try to involve them. In the middle of a sentence, I'll leave out a word and wait for a child to supply it. I also ask questions: "Now what do you think will happen?" And I read all the words, explaining any that might be unfamiliar. To make your reading lively, first spark your children's interest. Before you read a new book, let the youngsters study the cover. Ask what they see and what they think the book is about. Next point out the pictures in the book. Ask, "What do you think is happening here?" As you read, point out interesting pictures or characters. When you're finished, ask what the youngsters liked best about the story or how they would change the ending. This kind of active reading stimulates language development and encourages original thinking. A study by the State University of New York at Stony Brook found that preschool children whose parents read to them in an active, involved way tested six to eight months ahead of other children.

7. Finally, keep reading to them after they can read for themselves. Most children's listening comprehension is

much higher than their reading comprehension—so they get more out of hearing a book. Reading to older children also enables you to introduce books they might not explore on their own.[13]

About the same time she wrote the essay, Barbara began a ten-week series on the ABC radio network titled "Mrs. Bush's Story Time." She read from favorite books, offered reading tips, and interviewed celebrities.

Barbara says that the best time to start reading to children is "as soon as they will sit still, even for a minute." She fondly tells of the time that granddaughter Noelle, daughter of Jeb and Columba, informed her grandmother that "I love Moses."

"I was so surprised and said, 'Oh, really. Who was Moses?' Barbara said. "She didn't have the slightest idea and couldn't say why she loved him. So I got some books on Moses and then she really did love him."[14]

In June of 1991 Barbara delivered the commencement address at a vocational high school in the Bronx. She told graduates of Grace H. Dodge that they were shining examples of what could be accomplished at a vocational school. And she urged them to go back into their rough neighborhoods and help those who have been left behind.

The advice she gave them was similar to what she tells audiences wherever she goes—get involved, help someone in greater need than yourself.

"Counsel teenagers on the edge, comfort parents who have lost their own children to violence, drugs, or despair," she said.

"And if and when you have your own children, love them, listen to them, read to them, be gentle with them, put them first . . . show them how to care for others—that's the greatest gift you can give."

Epilogue

When Barbara leaves the White House, she knows precisely what she wants to do—get a house in Houston, spend more time on the edge of the Atlantic Ocean at Kennebunkport, Maine, relax with her grandchildren, and spend long mornings in the garden.

Of course, being married to George Bush, she no doubt will still do mega amounts of entertaining, and that's all right with her.

The Bushes haven't made a final decision yet on just where in Houston they will settle in retirement. They own a vacant lot there located right between two longtime friends, Marion Chambers and Bobby Fitch. Barbara had considered building a house on the property, but she said in 1991 that she no longer thought that was such a good idea.

"It occurs to me that is not the most brilliant thing in the world to do," she said. "We love them both so . . . how do I know they're going to get along with each other and I'm in the middle."

Another problem with building a house is that it takes a long time, and George Bush likes to get life rolling right away when he moves. Barbara still hasn't forgotten the time he invited King Hussein of Jordan to dinner before they even had a house.

So, she said, "I'd like to go home and buy a little house."

Only one of the Bush children, George W., lives in Texas, so the family will still be scattered once the senior Bushes retire. Both Marvin and Doro live in Washington, but Doro may leave the city when her parents depart.

Wherever they are in the winter months, it is likely the entire Bush clan will continue to get together at Kennebunkport in late summer. Barbara and George bought a house on Walker's Point from George's aunt in 1980 to make sure it remained in the family. The property was damaged extensively during a storm late in 1991, but the Bushes plan to rebuild and repair.

If George Bush serves a full second term in the White House, Barbara will be seventy-two years old when they leave Washington. She has expressed fears in the past that she will be too old by that time to fully take part in the activities she so enjoys.

But Barbara has never been the kind of woman who spends much time on regrets. Life for her, whether at the White House, in Maine, or in Texas, is always full speed ahead, with as much fun and fellowship along the way as she can muster.

Notes

CHAPTER 1

1. Quoted in Susan Baer, "Lady Flap," *Baltimore Sun,* April 27, 1990, p. 1F, 5F.

2. Ibid.

3. "Barbara Bush and the Norms of '47," *New York Times,* June 1, 1990, Editorial Page.

4. Ellen Goodman, "A Proper Match for Commencement Day," *Boston Globe,* April 22, 1990, p. A27.

5. Peggy Reid, "We Didn't Criticize Mrs. Bush," *New York Times,* May 16, 1990, p. A27.

6. David Stoughton, "Wellesley Class," *Los Angeles Times,* May 21, 1990, p. 6.

7. Kenneth Walsh, "The Hidden Life of Barbara Bush," *U.S. News & World Report,* May 28, 1990, pp. 25–27.

8. Associated Press, "Wellesley Students Hail Raisa Gorbachev," *New York Times,* May 20, 1990, p. 26.

9. Tom Shales, "Cameras on the Commencement," *Washington Post,* June 2, 1990, p. C1.

10. Fox Butterfield, "Family First, Mrs. Bush Tells Friend and Foe at Wellesley," *New York Times,* June 2, 1990, p. 5.

11. Rania Nagulb, "First Lady's Speech," *Los Angeles Times,* June 8, 1990, p. B6.

12. Quoted in Paula Chin, "In the Eye of the Storm," *People,* Oct., 1990, p. 84.

13. Quoted in Marian Christy, "Jamie Bush Sees Love, Strength at White House," *Boston Globe,* Feb. 26, 1991, p. 58.

14. Quoted in Barbara Feinman, "Barbara Bush's Entertaining Secrets," *Washington Post,* Nov. 14, 1989, p. B6.

CHAPTER 2

1. Quoted in Donnie Radcliffe, *Simply Barbara Bush* (New York: Warner Books, 1989), p. 73.

2. Cory Servaas, "Our Healthy Veep and Family," *Saturday Evening Post,* October 1988, pp. 46–47.

3. Quoted in Radcliffe, *Simply Barbara Bush,* p. 79.

4. Quoted in Frank P. Jarrell, "Former Student in Limelight," *The News and Courier,* Charleston, South Carolina, Feb. 10, 1980.

CHAPTER 3

1. George Bush with Victor Gold, *Looking Forward* (New York: Doubleday, 1987), p. 31.

2. Quoted in Patricia McCarthy, "Barbara Bush Addresses Ashley Hall Graduates," *The News and Courier,* Charleston, South Carolina, June 4, 1984.

3. Quoted in Joe Hyams, *Flight of the Avenger* (New York: Harcourt Brace Jovanovich, 1991), p. 55.

4. Smith College, *Associates News,* Nov. 5, 1943, p. 2.

5. Quoted in Hyams, *Flight of the Avenger,* p. 68.

6. George Bush with Victor Gold, *Looking Forward,* p. 23.

7. Quoted in Cathleen Decker, "Stalwart Hub of the Family—Barbara Bush: Loyal Wife Who's Reserved, Not Shy," *Los Angeles Times,* Aug. 7, 1988, p. 1.

CHAPTER 4

1. George Bush, "Texas 1948: Some Fond Memories," *American West,* January–February 1986, p. 37.

2. Quoted in Jean Libman Block, "The Best Time of My Life Is Now," *Good Housekeeping,* November 1989, p. 255.

3. Quoted in Donnie Radcliffe, *Simply Barbara Bush* (New York: Warner Books, 1989), p. 111.

4. Quoted in Jean Becker, "Well-Traveled Bush Grew Up in Oilfields," *USA Today,* April 5, 1988, p. 8A.

5. Quoted in Kathy Lewis, "Hospital Visit Evokes Memories of Bushes' Tragedy," *Houston Post,* June 29, 1986, p. 1A.

6. Quoted in Doug Wead, *George Bush, Man of Integrity,* (Eugene, Oregon: Harvest House, 1988), pp. 46–47.

7. Quoted in Radcliffe, *Simply Barbara Bush,* p. 119.

CHAPTER 5

1. Quoted in Doug Wead, *George Bush, Man of Integrity* (Eugene, Oregon: Harvest House, 1988), p. 118.

2. Quoted in Jean Libman Block, "The Best Time of My Life Is Now," *Good Housekeeping,* November 1989, p. 255.

3. Quoted in Betsy Cuniberti, "Return of the First Family," *Los Angeles Times,* Nov. 20, 1988, p. 1 View Section.

4. Quoted in David Maraniss, "The Bush Bunch," *Washington Post* magazine, Jan. 22, 1989, p. 14.

5. Ibid.

6. Quoted in Susan Schindehette, "A First Family that Just Won't Quit," *People,* Jan. 30, 1989, p. 63.

7. Marvin Bush, "My Second Chance," *Ladies Home Journal,* March 1989, p. 193.

8. Quoted in Cory Servaas, "Our Healthy Veep and Family," *Saturday Evening Post,* October 1988, pp. 71–72.

9. Quoted in *Good Housekeeping,* April 1989, p. 233. No byline.

10. Quoted in Cindy Adams, "Barbara Bush—First Lady, First Class," *Ladies Home Journal,* November 1990, p. 276.

CHAPTER 6

1. Quoted in Cindy Adams, "Barbara Bush," *Ladies Home Journal,* October 1988, p. 154.

2. George Bush with Victor Gold, *Looking Forward,* (New York: Doubleday, 1987), p. 101.

3. Quoted in Cindy Adams, "At Home with George and Barbara Bush," *Ladies Home Journal,* July 1986, p. 130.

4. Quoted in Doug Wead, *George Bush, Man of Integrity* (Eugene, Oregon: Harvest House, 1988), p. 136.

5. Quoted in Kenneth T. Walsh, "The Hidden Life of Barbara Bush," *U.S. News & World Report,* May 28, 1990, pp. 25–26.

CHAPTER 7

1. Quoted in Donnie Radcliffe, *Simply Barbara Bush,* (New York: Warner Books, 1989), p. 57.

2. Quoted in Douglas Kneeland, "Man in the News George Herbert Walker Bush," *New York Times,* Nov. 6, 1980, p. A25.

3. Quoted in Joyce Purnick, "Barbara Bush: Supportive Wife, Not a Maker of Political Waves," *New York Times,* July 18, 1980, p. A10.

4. Quoted in Betty Beale, "Barbara Bush Enjoys Race," *Washington Star,* Oct. 19, 1980.

5. Quoted in Donnie Radcliffe, "For Barbara Bush, Seconds Count," *Washington Post,* Oct. 18, 1980. p. B5.

CHAPTER 8

1. Quoted in Gloria Borger, "Who Is She? Second Lady Barbara Bush," *Savvy,* August 1983, p. 43.

2. Quoted in Joy Billington, "The Independent Lady of the Other White House," *Washington Star,* March 8, 1981, p. G2.

3. Quoted in Gloria Borger, "Who Is She? Second Lady Barbara Bush," *Savvy,* August 1983, pp. 42–43.

4. Quoted in John Robinson, "Hands on Style in Kid Gloves," *Boston Globe,* Dec. 21, 1988, p. 1.

5. Quoted in Diane Casselberry Manuel, "Barbara Bush," *Christian Science Monitor,* July 10, 1984, p. 25.

6. Quoted in Marjorie Hunter, "Barbara Bush: Cheering on the Reagan Team," *New York Times,* April 25, 1982.

7. Quoted in Donnie Radcliffe, "Barbara Bush's Role," *Washington Post,* June 5, 1988. p. F4.

8. Quoted in Joan Nathan, "Barbara Bush Hosts a Tea Party," *McCall's,* May 7, 1986, pp. 129–132.

CHAPTER 9

1. Quoted in Kathy Lewis, "The Big Prize: Going for the Presidency," *Houston Post,* Oct. 11, 1987, p. 20A.

2. Barbara Bush and Jean Becker, "Barbara Can't Wait to Join the Party," *USA Today,* Aug. 15, 1988, p. 4A.

3. Barbara Bush and Jean Becker, "Barbara's Closing the Maine House," *USA Today,* Aug. 16, 1988, p. 4A.

4. Quoted in Donnie Radcliffe, "On the Hustings with Barbara and Kitty," *Washington Post,* Oct. 30, 1988, p. F6.

5. Barbara Bush and Jean Becker, "Stars Join Candidates on the Campaign Trail," *USA Today,* Oct. 17, 1988, p. 13A.

6. Quoted in Carol Horner, "Barbara Bush—Speaking Her Mind," *Philadelphia Inquirer,* Oct. 23, 1988, p. K1.

7. Quoted in David Kaplan, "Barbara Bush Stands by Her Man," *Houston Post,* Oct. 16, 1988, p. G1.

8. Quoted in Sue Reilly, "The Candidates for First Lady," *Los Angeles Daily News,* Oct. 19, 1988.

9. Barbara Bush and Jean Becker, "Dinners with Friends Provide Campaign Breaks," *USA Today,* Oct. 31, 1988, p. 11A.

CHAPTER 10

1. Quoted in Thomas DeFrank and Ann McDaniels, "I've Got George Bush," *Newsweek,* Jan. 23, 1989, p. 25.

2. Quoted in Lois Romano, "Barbara Bush's Happy Hundred," *Washington Post,* May 2, 1989, p. D1.

3. Quoted in Kathy Lewis, "Partying Bush Style," *Houston Post,* May 17, 1989.

4. Quoted in Dodie Kazanjians, "The Bush Family Summers on Walker's Point," *House & Garden,* June 1989, pp. 141–144.

5. Quoted in Kathy Lewis, "Barbara Bush: The First 135 Days," *Houston Post,* June 4, 1989, p. F1.

6. Quoted in Donnie Radcliffe, "Barbara Bush and Her Freshman Year," *Washington Post,* Jan. 21, 1990, p. F1.

CHAPTER 11

1. Quoted in Paula Chin, "In the Eye of the Storm," *People,* October 1990, p. 84.

2. Quoted in Donnie Radcliffe, "Barbara Bush's Pilgrimage," *Washington Post,* Nov. 23, 1990, p. C4.

3. Quoted in Landon Jones and Maria Wilhelm, "Tough and Tender Talk," *People,* Dec. 17, 1990, p. 49.

4. Ibid. p. 50.

CHAPTER 12

1. Quoted in Kathy Lewis, "Bushes Learn Africans Have Abundance of Tears, Woes," *Houston Post,* March 17, 1985, p. 1A.

2. Ibid.

3. Quoted in Cindy Adams, "At Home with George and Barbara Bush," *Ladies Home Journal,* July 1986, p. 131.

4. Quoted in Donnie Radcliffe, "The First Lady Abroad," *Washington Post,* Feb. 1, 1989, p. B8.

5. Ann McFeatters, "Barbara Bush in Europe," *Scripps Howard News Service,* June 2, 1989.

6. Quoted in Donnie Radcliffe, "Barbara Bush on the Role Not Taken," *Washington Post,* July 17, 1989, p. B1.

CHAPTER 13

1. Quoted in Cory Servaas, "Our Healthy Veep and Family," *Saturday Evening Post,* October 1988, pp. 48–49.

2. Quoted in John Ensor Harr, "The Crusade Against Illiteracy," *Saturday Evening Post,* December 1988, pp. 43–44.

3. Quoted in Gloria Borger, "Who Is She? Second Lady Barbara Bush," *Savvy,* August 1983, p. 42.

4. Quoted in Marian Christy, "Jamie Bush Sees Love, Strength at White House," *Boston Globe,* Feb. 26, 1991, p. 51.

5. Quoted in Trude B. Feldman, "George and Barbara Bush," *McCall's,* September 1988, p. 83.

6. Barbara Bush with Jean Becker, "Meeting Great People Up North and Down South," *USA Today,* Oct. 3, 1988, p. 9A.

7. Quoted in Donnie Radcliffe, "For Barbara Bush, Hearts and Hands at Washington Home," *Washington Post,* Feb. 15, 1989, p. C1.

8. Quoted in Edward Klein, "Everything Would be Better," *Parade,* May 21, 1989, p. 4.

9. Quoted in Lois Romano, "The Hug that Speaks for Itself," *Washington Post,* March 23, 1989, p. D5.

10. Quoted in Art Harris, "Mrs. Bush's Private Lesson," *Washington Post,* May 15, 1989, p. C4.

11. Quoted in Barbara Kantrowitz and Ann McDaniel, "A First Lady Who Cares," *Newsweek,* July 10, 1989. p. 44.

12. Quoted in Jean Libman Block, "The Best Time of My Life Is Now," *Good Housekeeping,* November 1989, p. 254.

13. *Reader's Digest,* "Barbara Bush on Reading to Children," October 1990, as excerpted by Scripps Howard News Service, Sept. 5, 1990.

14. Quoted in Jim Brosseau, "When Barbara Bush Reads Babar," *New Choices,* May 1990, p. 71.

Index

237